Fundamentals of Model Boat Building

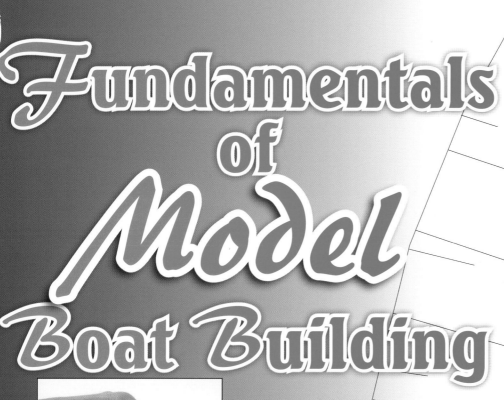

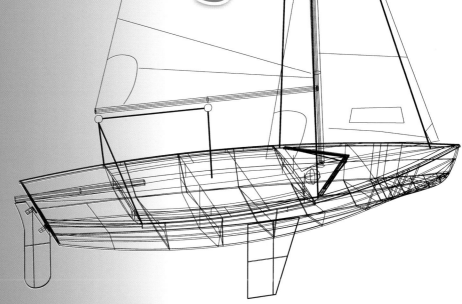

John Into & Nancy Price

Schiffer Publishing Ltd

4880 Lower Valley Road, Atglen, Pennsylvania 19310

Dedication

To all of our parents and family, who each contributed in their own way to our unusual view of the world.

Acknowledgments

We would like to thank the following people: David and Ann Phillips for their moral support, Irv from Connecticut, who taught us to appreciate what fixturing is and to Ray Weinstock who has been here to help even when he didn't know it. And of course... To Bill and Shannon...

Disclaimer and Acknowledgment of Trademarks

Most of the items and products in this book may be covered by various copyrights, trademarks, and logotypes. Their use herein is for identification purposes only. All rights are reserved by their respective owners.

Other Schiffer Books on Related Subjects:
Model Boat Building. Steve Rogers and Patricia Staby Rogers. ISBN: 0764310704. $14.95
Model Boat Building Made Simple. Steve Rogers. ISBN: 0887403883. $12.95
Model Boat Building: The Skipjack. Steve Rogers & Patricia Staby-Rogers. ISBN: 0887409377. $14.95

Library of Congress Control Number: 2010937789

Designed by Mark David Bowyer
Type set in Seagull Hv BT / Humanist 521 BT

ISBN: 978-0-7643-3105-3
Printed in China

Schiffer Books are available at special discounts for bulk purchases for sales promotions or premiums. Special editions, including personalized covers, corporate imprints, and excerpts can be created in large quantities for special needs. For more information contact the publisher:

Published by Schiffer Publishing Ltd.
4880 Lower Valley Road
Atglen, PA 19310
Phone: (610) 593-1777; Fax: (610) 593-2002
E-mail: Info@schifferbooks.com

For the largest selection of fine reference books on this and related subjects, please visit our web site at
www.schifferbooks.com
We are always looking for people to write books on new and related subjects. If you have an idea for a book please contact us at the above address.

This book may be purchased from the publisher.
Include $5.00 for shipping.
Please try your bookstore first.
You may write for a free catalog.

In Europe, Schiffer books are distributed by
Bushwood Books
6 Marksbury Ave.
Kew Gardens
Surrey TW9 4JF England
Phone: 44 (0) 20 8392 8585; Fax: 44 (0) 20 8392 9876
E-mail: info@bushwoodbooks.co.uk
Website: www.bushwoodbooks.co.uk

Contents

Introduction

The building of model boats is an interesting mix of art and technology. As an art, any method, any material, and any interpretation are allowed. Model making is sculpture, usually multi-media sculpture. It is always an interpretation of the original subject by its artist. Very, very rarely is it actually an exact miniature of the subject. As with all art, judgment by others will be in the eye of the beholder.

Model makers are usually, but not always, expected to make their models look as much like the original object as possible. This is a factor that creates a continuum between art and technology that has a certain tension to it. Interpretation has infinite variability. A model can be accurate and yet be almost devoid of detail. Such is the case with lines models. Minimizing details does not make a model incorrect. Maximizing details certainly makes it more comprehensive, but not more correct. Quantity is not the same thing as quality.

With art, there are many paintings that we might all agree look like the subject in them. Do they really? If you strip them down to their technique and materials, or should I say, if you understand its creative process too well, do you see the image, or its constituent parts? For the most part, I think that artists hope it is the former and I think for the most part that is the case. If we look at cartoon artistry, we see that a simple line sketch with a few exaggerated features can be drawn that we can immediately recognize as a famous politician or movie star. Again, the eye of the beholder determines how much this is so, but it shows that there are ways of presenting and creating things that may be simpler and more elegant than we imagine until we allow ourselves some expressive freedom. A door can be shown by four thin lines with a circle for a doorknob. You will see this is done in thousands of old ship models. Is it the best way? The choice belongs to you alone, the artist. Does the beholder agree? If they are not making the model, it's not their choice. The fact is that they probably didn't even notice; perhaps they had no idea that the door was not a real miniature, when placed in context with the overall model.

A lot of making things look real comes from allowing oneself to be an artist. The greatest models in the world contain much that is suggestive and in some cases, downright illusion. Never confuse this with taking shortcuts or having a disregard for quality. Instead, bear in mind that as a modeler and artist, you have an open palette. What you know now and what you learn are all things that you can use to make magic. There are so many things that can go into a model that they can be interpreted in a million different ways that are all "correct."

Model makers use elements of engineering. A model is, after all, a physical entity. Engineers design things to function. They design things using languages that pertain to their specialties. They must communicate with each other via terminology and via visual information, especially drawings. You will find in making models that you, as the recorder of information, must draw up your information in such a way that a different version of yourself, the chief carpenter, must understand, perhaps many months later, when working in the shop. For this reason, we teach you to understand mechanical drawings.

Engineers are also concerned with working precisely. For them, this attention to precision makes all of the difference between the success and failure of their designs. Where an engineer's concern with precision is sometimes a matter of life and death, it is not so for the modeler. However, a model maker's attention to precision does make all of the difference in both dimensional accuracy and aesthetics. For this reason, we will teach you about special measuring techniques and tools.

Both engineers and artists are concerned with materials, their properties, their interactions, and how to work with them. You will find much discussion about this, especially when we discuss carving theory.

In society, artists and engineers often see themselves at polar ends of the spectrum of philosophies about the world. In a very generic sense they are doing the same thing: They are all working towards the creation of things that are special. As model makers, our goal is the same.

We have been lucky to have grown up with and to have been influenced strongly by members of both the artistic and engineering spheres in our immediate families, our widespread group of beloved friends and in those who have been our mentors. In fact many of these people have also worked and trained in other professions and have a wide variety of philosophies about a lot of things. We, ourselves, also have other professional education and experiences of our own. Because of the virtually limitless way that models can be expressed, all of these things can play a part in how that expression is made and can play a part in solving the many puzzles of which a model is comprised.

One of the great things about learning to make models is a realization that the vast collection of knowledge that it can embody is like a large pot of soup. Any experience, knowledge or skill can be thrown in to make it better. Model making is not any one skill or process. What do you bring to it already? There is likely to be much more at your disposal than you might think.

When we wrote this book, it was with the knowledge that we have no idea what your skill level is. You may have made many models. On the other hand, you may just be wondering how it's done. It doesn't matter. Because of all the possibilities and all of the different types of knowledge that go into this soup, nobody knows all there is to know. We hope that our two cents worth will help you in whatever way you plan to enjoy model making.

There is a lot of information in this book. It is not about building one specific model of one specific boat, to the exclusion of others. We did not intend for it to. Rather it is the start of a series of books that are meant to teach you the skills to be a model maker, so that you can develop and hone your craftsmanship.

Because we are making models of boats, we need to start at the core of any boat: the hull. It is the foundation of all boats. It is usually, although not always, the most complicated single structure in a boat. This is because of such factors as compound curves, structural concepts, unusual terminology, measurement concepts, and a few other things. The hull is the foundation for all other parts, which are either built into it later, or somehow attached. Hulls are defined by what the boat must do and what it faces when it does it.

The lines of any boat hull are the essence of its shape and carry with them the original designers intent of making that boat capable of doing what it has to do. It's lines are often enough to define the type of boat, without any other details shown. This is the significant element in making half hull models. Being able to capture the hull's essence in this way provides a foundation that can be as beneficial to your overall model as a real boat's hull is important to its function. Whether your model is going to be minimalist or highly detailed, its overall beauty and "truthfulness" will be much greater if you start with a well-made and accurate hull.

There is a lot that we have to share with you. Much more than can be put into one, or even a few books on this subject. We believe that this book hits on some very important fundamentals and has information for model makers of all levels. You will find that many things are presented as theory: we believe that this is unusual with this type of book. Theory teaches you why things are done the way they are, as opposed to telling you what to do. We believe that if you understand the reason for doing things, you can better apply these things to the project you want to do, not just the one that we choose for you.

Regardless of any other factors, the building of scratch built models is highly dependent upon your own desire and ingenuity. Put this together with the information here and you will have all you need to start the process of making the boat of your own choosing.

Good luck!

Chapter 1
Learning to Think Like a Model Maker

Nancy and I are professional model makers. Our primary subjects are boats. We have now made well over three hundred models. We design and make *every single piece* of every model that we create. Because of the things that we have learned over the years, we can now make a scratch built model of any vessel that we can either get sufficient information about or access to. As a result, we are often called upon to make models of unusual boats.

We exhibit our models at a lot of shows throughout the United States, especially at boat shows. It's fun to meet all sorts of interesting people and to spend time around and on different types of boats. Among the people we meet are other model makers who want to exchange ideas. Some of them want to know our "secrets." We also meet many people who are just starting out with model making and are looking for some direction about where to learn more about how to make them. A lot of questions that we get reveal to us that for many people model making can be mysterious and almost impossible to fathom.

Occasionally we have families walk by our display and a member of the group will loudly whisper "daddy will make you a much nicer model when we get home," apparently in the belief that there is nothing to it. More than a few times, the father who was "set up" in that situation has returned to us the following year to say: " I started with a piece of wood and tried to make a model, but that's as far as I could get...". This is a time when some people realize that there is more to making models than meets the eye.

Figure 1. Tom Donley's *RETROSPECT*, one of our antique & classic models. Tom has lent his model for us to display at many of the shows that we go to. It is a 1958 Century Coronado, a very elegant and "state of the art" boat in its time. *Courtesy of Tom Donley*.

Models make us think of things that we enjoyed as children and we have found that there are many people who firmly believe that making models should be an activity limited strictly to children. While many of us enjoyed seeing and playing with models as children, those of us who put them together usually did so from very basic kits. Very few of us actually tried to create realistic models from scratch when we were children, except in the rare case, that there was a mentor to provide guidance. Thus, it seems that some people have a notion that making models from scratch is innate, simple, and a sign of immaturity. As you learn to create serious models, you will find that it involves learning concepts and skills that are not so innate and, in fact, serious model making requires the practice of some skills that virtually define maturity, such as patience, persistence, the ability to discern accuracy and quality, and the ability to develop strategic plans. You are very unlikely to find a good model builder who does not take great pride in what he or she does.

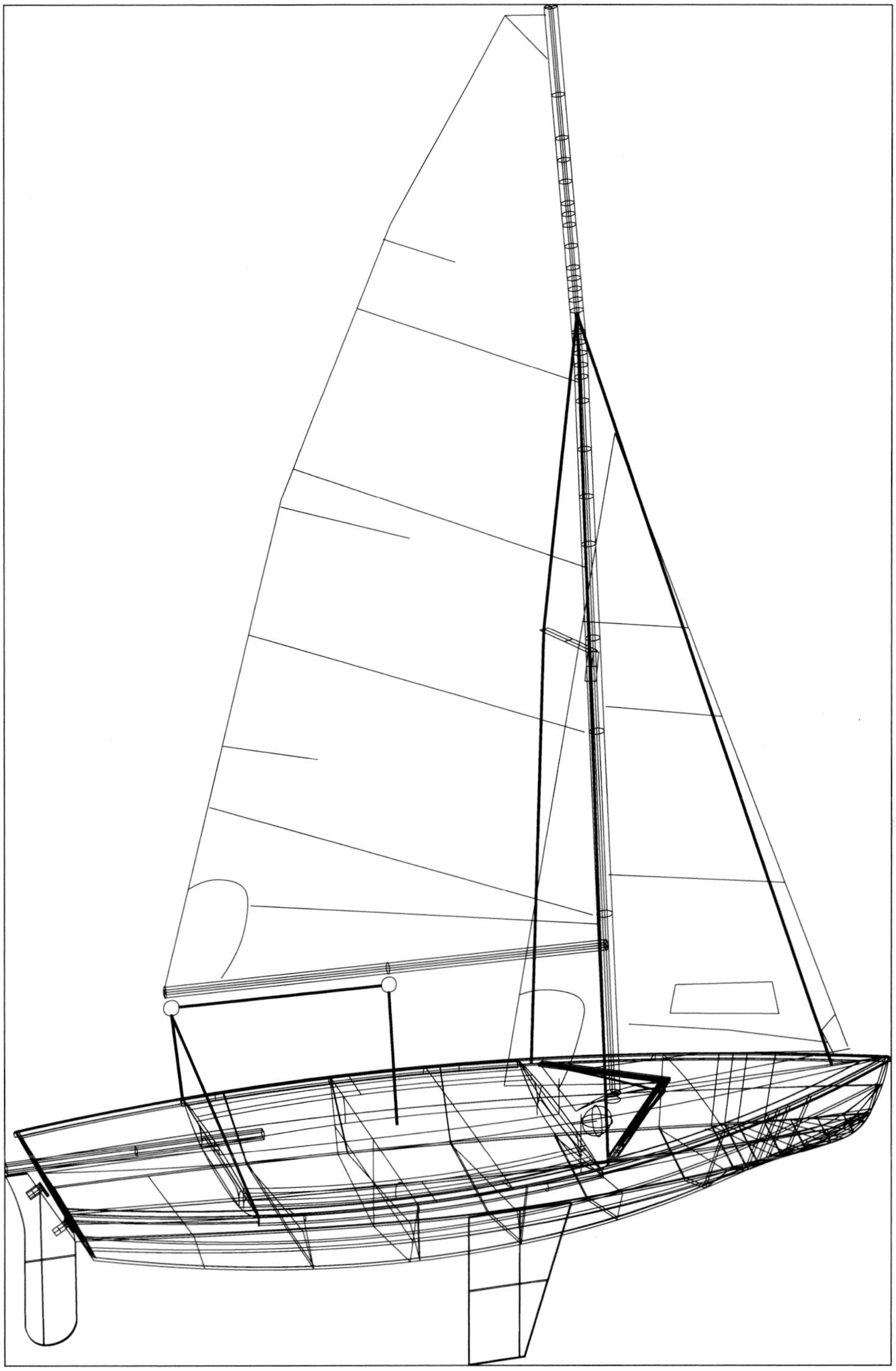

When I started making models from kits, almost fifty years ago, I had few problems with most beginner's models, but it was very hard and sometimes impossible to finish what I perceived to be more difficult models that I now realize were just as basic. The reason for this was simple: I had no clue about what I was doing. The easier models were simply those with instructions that gave me more information. I really knew nothing about how one goes about making a model; I had no clear idea how it is constructed or what end goal I was supposed to be achieving. I was simply following a recipe. If I could follow the recipe, I was successful. If not, I was stuck. I was in the same situation as the guy whose family expected him to come up with a model out of thin air. Experience has taught me that we are not born with this knowledge, so I am no longer embarrassed to admit that I didn't know what I needed to back then: It is impossible to know what you don't know. It took a long time and a lot of mistakes to get to the point where I understood that there were things that I needed to learn and what they were.

Figure 2. Such design work is not exactly child's play, but models can, and should, bring out the child in all of us. A perspective drawing from our plans for a Snipe sailboat model.

As you build more and more kits, you gain experience with some of the techniques that are commonly used and you may find that with greater practice you know what to do in situations where information isn't provided. This kind of practice is a great way to become a better model builder and your skills will improve with each kit that you tackle. Building models from kits is one of the best ways to gain exposure to the different ways that they can be created.

Building kits alone, however, will not teach you how to build models from scratch. If you happen to have other related skills or knowledge, for instance if you are someone who builds things for a living, you may have some advantages, but a kit alone is not going to give you all of the information you need. What a kit does is to provide you with a recipe, the materials, and usually at least one picture of what your model should look like when it's done. It is important that you do everything step by step and, if you miss a step, you could have problems down the road, sometimes serious, especially if you don't understand the cause.

Figure 3. Our subject boat: the Chesapeake Deadrise *ANNIE BUCK*.
Courtesy of David and Ann Phillips.

To make a scratch-built model means to start with drawings and raw materials and to create the model from your own ideas and plans. That is, you are the creator of the recipe. There are several advantages to being able to build from scratch, the most obvious being that you can choose which boat will be your subject without relying on whether or not there is a kit of that boat available. Other advantages include that you have total control of such options as size, style, and the amount of detail that you want to give it. Another important one is that, because you are the one planning the outcome, which means that you understand the process the entire way through, you have full control over the end product of your work and, if at some point you want to change something, you can do it. I don't want to fail to mention the kind of satisfaction that you will feel when you have made your own model starting from your first imaginings and ending with a 3-dimensional work that you created yourself.

If your preference is building kits, you'll find that once you understand the information in these pages, you should have the ability to analyze your kit and have a better understanding of how and why the model was designed in the way it was, what procedures are critical and in what order, and how to improve on, or even change, the kit to suit your desires. After all, the designer of that kit initially built it from scratch.

You will notice that we only concentrate on one particular boat in this book: the *ANNIE BUCK*. The *ANNIE BUCK* is a Chesapeake Bay Deadrise and is a boat that we know very well. One thing that we want you to understand is that there are many ways to make models and this point will become all the clearer, because we use only one boat as a subject, rather than several. You will see that you can make a model of almost any boat in many different ways and that what limits your abilities has relatively little to do with what the subject boat is and much more to do with what is in your repertoire, both in terms of what you can imagine and in terms of your abilities. Looking at different ways of approaching the same boat will increase your repertoire tremendously. A Deadrise has features common to a lot of boats, which makes it an excellent subject for this book. As you learn the techniques we use on the *ANNIE BUCK*, you will begin to see how the same methods can be used with other boats, too.

What I am able to do now, that I couldn't back when I "had no clue about what I was doing," is to "think like a model maker." Simply put, this means that when I look at a potential subject boat I can see, in my mind, ways to make a model of that boat including potential methods of construction and possible materials to use for that construction. It means that I have a fairly good sense of the boat's shape and why it has that shape. It means that I can see particular features that are important to it. It means that I can envision it as a model.

After you've read through this book and practiced with some of your own models we hope that you too will learn to "think like a model maker" when you look at a boat. When you have reached the point where you can do so confidently, you will know that you have actually become a model maker.

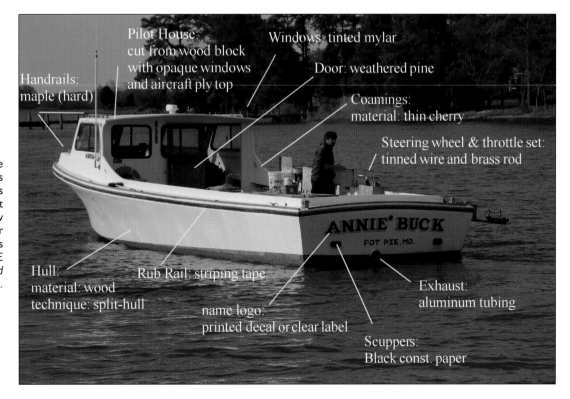

Figure 4. Thinking like a model maker means envisioning possibilities when looking at subject boats. These notes show possible materials for representing various parts of the *ANNIE BUCK*. Courtesy of David and Ann Phillips.

Pilot House: cut from wood block with opaque windows and aircraft ply top

Windows: tinted mylar

Door: weathered pine

Handrails: maple (hard)

Coamings: material: thin cherry

Steering wheel & throttle set: tinned wire and brass rod

Hull: material: wood technique: split-hull

Rub Rail: striping tape

name logo: printed decal or clear label

Exhaust: aluminum tubing

Scuppers: Black const. paper

ANNIE BUCK
POT PIE. MD.

Chapter 2
Model Variations

Not only are models not things that only belong to the domain of children, they have a much larger presence in our lives than we probably realize. When we hear the word model, we may immediately think of a toy or a radio controlled miniature. These are models that appeal to the child in us: something that we should never lose. We are actually surrounded everywhere by models without really being aware of it.

Models have been around for centuries. As miniatures of real objects, they are often used as industrial prototypes. Architects use them to show what a single room or a whole city would look like. Submissions to the U.S. Patent Office have always been made in one of two ways: mechanical drawing or physical model.

In marketing, models are used to present prototypes from idea to investor and from there into the showroom. Did you know that they make models of beer bottles to see what they will look like before you do? We all know that models are used in the movies to represent real things that are either too expensive to make at full size or that are destined to be destroyed.

Figure 1. Technology has come a long way in the last century. An image like this proposal rendering for a model is enough to be considered a model for some purposes. This is because of the accuracy and powers of CAD, or Computer Aided Drafting.

Models are also used in industry to test physical properties. In the aerospace, automobile, and other industries they are used to test aerodynamics, hydrodynamics, and other performance characteristics. You sometimes see pictures of models of cars or airplanes in wind tunnels. In the same way that aircraft models are used for testing in wind tunnels, boat hull models are tested in water tanks.

In medicine, models are used as teaching objects. You can often see some excellent and really grotesque versions when you visit your veterinarian's office.

In museums and other educational settings, models are used to preserve history. Models that are accurate visual representations of historically significant subjects can show what a boat, car, airplane or any other physical object was like in three dimensions, presenting more information than photographs alone.

Figure 2. The *Marsc-Hen* is a modern style cabin cruiser based upon a traditional lobster boat design. Our model would be considered to be moderately highly detailed. *Courtesy of Carl Baxter.*

Figure 3. This view of the *Marsc-Hen* shows the upholstery, instrumentation, trim tabs, and a partial view of its five-bladed propeller. *Courtesy of Carl Baxter.*

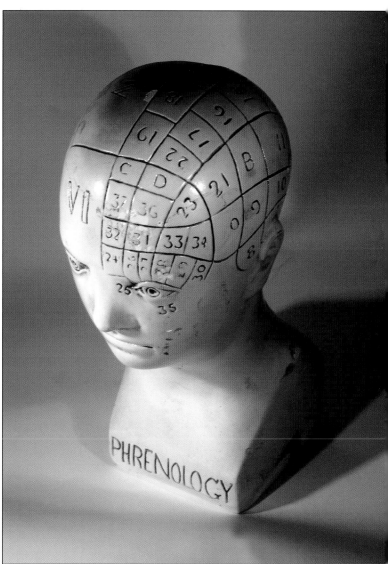

Figure 4. Various types of models are used in medicine and other scientific disciplines.

In the history of Naval Architecture, the design of boats, we often find that models were built to the designer's specifications. Only when a model's shape was satisfactory were the lines taken from it to build a full-sized ship. Lift-built half hulls were extensively used for this purpose. We will discuss lift-building as we look at methods of model construction. Other types of models were used in the design of sail plans and to determine the placement of plates on iron hulled vessels.

There are many ways to construct models, as we will see throughout this book. Why they are constructed in the ways that they are has to do with the type of boat being represented, tradition, the material resources and skills of the model maker, whim, and/or a variety of other reasons.

Any method that is used for making a full-sized boat can be used to make a model.

In addition to their type of construction, models are designed to have aesthetically different visual styles. This pertains not only to the model itself, but also to how it is displayed. While construction techniques may be dependent upon style and vice versa, the two are separate concepts. Models can be extremely detailed or not. They may be simple "lines" models, which are minimalist objects whose primary purpose is to show the shape of the hull and little else. Minimalism means to reduce something to the fewest features that define its essence well. Half-hulls are a style of display that often minimizes features in order to highlight the shape of the hull.

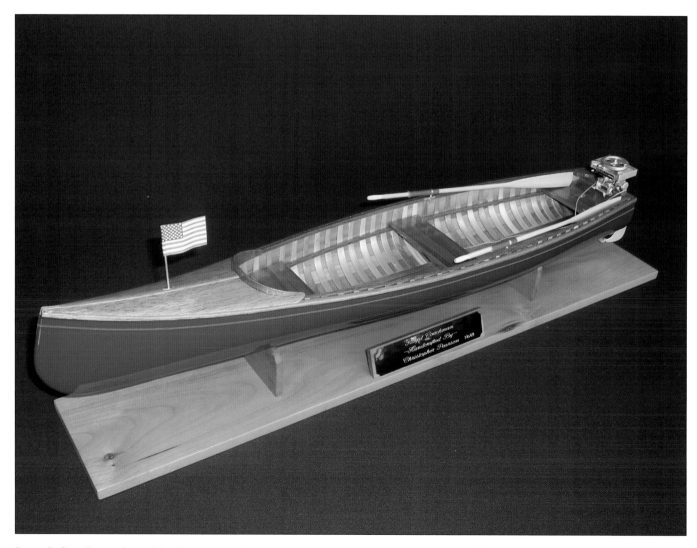

Figure 5. Chris Pearson's models of canoes are extremely accurate and will show people for generations to come what a particular canoe really looked like. This is a model of the *Royal Coachman*. *Photo courtesy of Christopher Pearson.*

Half-hulls can also be extremely detailed. Although most are made at lengths between one and four feet long, we have seen half-hulls that were over twenty-five feet long. Common subjects for half-hulls are America's Cup sailboats and merchant ships from the 1800s. In recent years, half hulls of newer fiberglass boats have also become popular. Most half hulls are mounted on wooden back plates, but sometimes they are mounted on mirrors, which creates the illusion of seeing a full hull model.

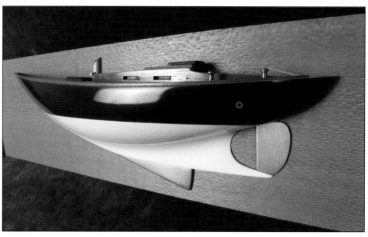

Figure 7. Another of my great uncle's half hulls: This one is yet to be identified, the customary labels having fallen from the backing board.

Figure 6. A half hull of the America's Cup defender *Weatherly*. This model was made by my great uncle, Grover Into.

Figure 8. This rare and wonderful model came to us for restoration. It is a "shadow box" diorama. It was probably made in the late 1800s or very early 1900s. The model is both a half hull and a waterline model.

Waterline models are flat at the boat's displacement waterline. They are meant to be placed on a flat tabletop or on a surface that has the appearance of water. There are some who feel that a model is not complete unless it includes the entire hull and other underwater features. Proponents of waterline models, on the other hand, contend that because, the model shows the boat as it would appear when in the water, it is more realistic. I do have to admit that I have never seen a real boat with brass pins supporting it. With waterline models, you can increase the realism of your display by adding piers, buoys or other environmental objects that add to the illusion that it is sitting in the water.

Dioramas are displays that miniaturize, not only a single object, but all of the various things within a given area. The large train displays one sees at Christmas time are dioramas. Some dioramas are of whole towns and cities. Harbor dioramas may include water, piers, buildings, vegetation, and, in some cases, underwater features including fish. I have seen dioramas that consist of a boat builder's shop including a marine railway and all of the boat builder's tools on the shop's walls. The boat is in the center of the building on a cradle. This is a powerful way of enhancing a model and showing off one's model making skills.

Of course, functional models including R/C (radio controlled) and pond yachts are among the most popular styles of model. They may be tremendously intricate, or meant solely for the pleasure of a cruise on a sunny Sunday afternoon. There are serious competitions between R/C'ers all over the world. There are miniature yacht clubs devoted to the sport. Versions of these boats range from rowing dinghies with moving rowers, dogs and ducks in pursuit to aircraft carriers, supertankers and submarines, to elegant sailing yachts. Pond models can be, but are not always R/C and may be operated simply by presetting the sails and holding on with a string.

Figure 10. I believe that this would be characterized as a model. Would you see it as a model if you knew that the protrusion below the motor is meant to attach it to a tree, because it happens to be one of many light covers from a string of holiday lights? You may be in the midst of models that you didn't realize are in the same room with you.

Figure 9. The *Oldsquaw* is a Chesapeake Bay Draketail. This is a basic split-hull waterline model. We have created a mini diorama by adding a base of painted acrylic "water" and a scale model of a pier.

Chapter 3
Mind Set

While it may seem strange to discuss how to think about things and how to prepare oneself mentally, you will find that some of the toughest impediments to successful model making come from our own tendencies to limit our vision of possibilities or from beliefs that we just don't have the "talent," or "patience," or some other characteristic that is a requirement of a model maker. The real requirements are that you have a desire to make models, that you are willing to put in the necessary effort, that you remain open to learning new skills and that you use your imagination, understanding that it is a tool as important as any other.

Model making teaches you a lot about problem solving. It is impossible to make a scratch built model without solving problems. Actually, let's refer to it as solving puzzles, instead. I say this because, even though we are basically referring to the same thing, solving problems sounds like something negative, whereas solving the puzzles involved in a model's creation is very enjoyable.

If you think about solving puzzles of any kind you know that your success improves as you practice and as you increase the knowledge required for that particular type of puzzle. Crossword puzzles teach you to increase your vocabulary, to learn how to see clues in the lining up of letters of adjoining words and that you shouldn't try to solve each word in the numerical sequence of the clue lists. Jigsaw puzzles require that you see and commit shapes to memory, learn to identify color clues, and that edge pieces are easier to identify than those in the middle.

When making a model from scratch you won't know what specific puzzles await you in advance. There are standard puzzles that have to be solved regardless of the boat, such as: What does the subject boat look like? What style of model would I like to make? What method of construction do I want to use? How detailed should it be? What size should it be? Am I sure that I want to do this? (*Just kidding*.)

These will be easy questions to answer once you have more information at your disposal. In fact, some of these puzzles are not so much puzzles as questions to be answered as a matter of preference.

Some of the most interesting puzzles develop in situations where you must find a way to make something that you've never tried before. You must come up with your own solution. Perhaps no one has ever done it before, but you have a gut feeling that you can come up with a way to do it and you become determined to make it happen. When you solve these types of puzzles, there's a very special feeling, because you might really be doing something original. I have found that these types of puzzles tend to become obsessions, as good puzzles usually do.

By studying the work of others, by spending time with other model makers, or by examination of any models that you have an opportunity to see up close, you can learn a lot of things. Other model makers have had to solve most of the same puzzles as you do, perhaps with some other variation. You can often learn how someone else solved a puzzle similar to yours; sometimes you can't quite figure things out just from looking at their work. However, you may discover that your desire to solve a puzzle, plus what small information you could glean from what someone else did, leads you to your own unexpected and perhaps better method.

If you would like to improve your problem solving skills, practice making models. You will have no choice but to get better at solving problems in an enjoyable and satisfying way.

You will find that one of the side benefits of the kind of thinking that you must do when making models is that you improve your ability to teach yourself new things. Most model makers that I know would characterize themselves as being "self-taught" to a large degree.

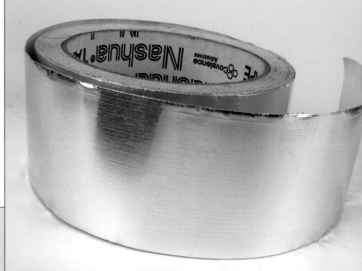

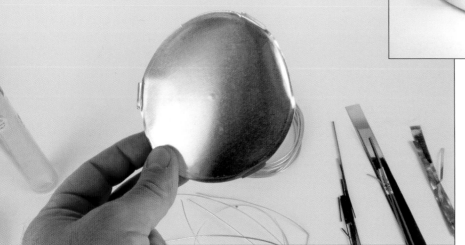

Figure 2. If you've done many kits, you will find that sometimes there are thin, self-adhesive metal parts that are used as trim for windshields, or for other items. They are usually made from the same material as the aluminum duct tape above. It can be applied to parts made from non-metal materials and burnished (rubbed) to make those objects look as though they are made from metal.

Figure 1. An example of a common type of puzzle that needs to be solved arises with the need to make metal parts, especially if your metal working facilities or abilities aren't the best. Does this look like metal? It's the inner lid from a peanut butter jar. It just happens to cut and behave like paper. Many things can be used by a model maker when viewed out of their normal context.

I can tell you that one secret to successfully solving many of the puzzles of model making is to free yourself, perhaps force yourself, to see things out of their common context. Bear in mind that although a model looks like the original subject, it is not the original subject. It is much smaller and, as a result, as much as you may want to build every single part in the same way as was done in the original, it is very rarely possible without some modifications. You will see that there are many reasons why.

This fact, that a model is a *model*, means that you should treat it as a model and not simply view it as a small boat. This fact can be used to your advantage, because materials and techniques can be used in a model that could never be used in an actual boat, in addition to the fact that any method used to make a boat can be used to make a model. This means there are many available solutions to your puzzles.

Of course you will want your model to be as much like the original as possible, especially in its appearance. On many occasions I have had to ask a client if it is more important to them that the model is constructed like the original or that it looks like the original. Usually the answer is the latter.

Figure 3. Some real metal products are easier to use than others. This chrome colored wire available at all craft stores. It is 22 gauge "tinned" wire.

Figure 4. With inexpensive bending pliers, which come in sets like this, you can use metal wire and bend it into all of the shapes shown here and hundreds of others. You can also hammer it flat to make other shapes. Many metal parts of boats can be fairly easily made with these techniques, but only if you can envision these possibilities. Each solution becomes a new part of your model-making repertoire.

Because a model is its own thing, there are myriad possibilities for materials that would never be used in the subject boat. When I tell people what I mean when I say to "see things out of their common context," some would say that I am nuts. Here are some examples: when you open a jar of peanut butter, or a package of cream cheese do you see the metallic film with its regularly spaced dimpled texture and say to yourself "hey, this looks like the face of a dashboard"? Do you see metal mesh holiday ribbon and think, "This looks like a miniature version of the screen that's used in a motor box vent"? Do you think about the fact that being true to scale means not only making objects smaller, but that your wood grain or fabric patterns should get smaller as well? Do you know that you can measure something by holding a piece of string next to it and making knots or marks at dimension points along with notes to accompany your string and properly measuring that string later, when you have the right tools available? Did you know that you could replicate painted sheet metal ductwork with heavy paper?

You may not find these particular examples exciting, unless they are the answers to your needs. They should demonstrate the point that rigidity in thinking can make it difficult to solve certain model making puzzles. You will likely miss opportunities and possibilities. This kind of thinking will come more easily for some people than others, but it is easy to develop with practice. If you start to worry that your ideas are getting a bit wild, there is no need to limit yourself; just don't tell anyone else what you are thinking.

After you solve your trickiest puzzle, don't just give your technique away either. On the one hand, it is your idea and you might want to let others work it out for themselves. There's nothing wrong with people asking themselves, "How did they do that?" Share your information with care.

More importantly, you should realize that our greatest power as model makers comes from the mystique that develops from the combination of the various illusions that we are creating when we use any of the techniques and materials that we do, especially those methods that weren't expected or are unorthodox. When the result is that someone looks at your model and sees, albeit only in their mind, the real boat and they forget for the moment that it is a model, it is doing what it is supposed to and you can not do anything better. You will find that the moment you tell the viewer how clever you were to make a winch from a sewing bobbin, you have broken the mystique; they are then seeing simply a model and worse, they may assume that they know all of your secrets! It wouldn't be true; however, the damage is done.

Figure 5. Everything in this image looks like metal. Almost any metal part of a boat can be made for a model using these materials, or using other non-metal parts in combination with these materials. Although not always obvious, there is always a solution.

If I had a penny for every time someone told us that we must be "so patient" … Yes, patience is good, but it is only a small aspect of what is important … and does not necessarily have anything to do with being either bored or in pain. Patience is best manifested in good organization of tasks. Watching paint or glue dry is not my idea of fun; on the other hand, neither is sanding and repainting or re-gluing work that did not have adequate time to dry or cure properly. There are so many things that have to be done while making a model that during the time that you are waiting for one thing, you can work on something else. It's good to try to learn not to think about the thing that is drying more than necessary (you do need to make periodic checks sometimes to make sure that the paint isn't developing drips). For paints or glues that call for overnight drying, plan that task so that it is the last one of the day so that it can thoroughly dry overnight. It will be ready for you when you start up again. The fact of the matter is that a model maker really doesn't spend much time doing nothing.

The corollary to patience that doesn't get as much press, and is really far more important, is persistence. I get sad when I think of the number of models that I quit, or almost quit working on when I was younger. It can be very hard when something doesn't work the way that you expected it to, especially when you don't know of a simple solution. This can be true whether you build models from scratch or from kits. If you break a part, it would seem that your kit is ruined. It's only true if you don't try to fix it. You really only have another puzzle. The questions to be answered in this puzzle are:

- Of what material is the part made?
- How do I get that material or is there a suitable substitute for it if I can't get the original material?
- How do I shape my new material into a replacement piece?

Thinking out of context (as we were just discussing):

- Is this piece required to finish the model and/or can I come up with another way to replace the function and/or appearance of it?

This latter approach will probably require a bit more research and effort to work out than simply replacing the original piece, but it is a way to save your model and you might even improve upon it. I like to approach every problem with the idea that if it has been solved before, there is a way that we can do it, too. We have very rarely been wrong.

If something you are working on makes you so frustrated that you get angry … ***stop***! Solutions require clear thinking. Anger gets in the way of thinking clearly as we all learn in some way at some point in time. While model making is usually quite relaxing, because you slowly mull over life and the problems of the world as you work, something that repeatedly does not work can also become a lightning rod for all of the other problems you are having. Coming back to the problem later on often reveals that the solution was not that tough. If you break something more, because anger took over, you will have that much more to fix.

One of the things that I learned as a student of psychology is a method that often helps me with some of my most difficult puzzles and when I am short on ideas. It may sound crazy, but don't knock it until you try it. Here it is.

Perhaps you've been in a situation where you run into someone familiar, but you can't actually remember who the person is. You hope against hope that they won't say something that would make you reveal that you can't remember who the mystery person is. You somehow managed to get through the situation undiscovered and then spend the next few hours trying to remember who he or she is.

You finally resign yourself to the fact that it will probably come to you late at night or early in the morning when you are lying awake. The strange thing is that it really does happen. Almost everyone has had such an experience. You cannot remember something during the day, or you have difficulty solving some nagging problem and are lying awake at night, and the answer, for some odd reason, pops into your head effortlessly!

Well, in sleep studies it has been found that there are various levels, or depths, of sleep. There are alpha, beta, and REM sleep levels. I am not going to try to explain things that I frankly don't remember that well in detail, but think of heavy sleep, light sleep, and a sort of semi-sleeping and semi-waking state, where your mind is working and thinking in an unencumbered way, while your body is still essentially sleeping. This may be between heavy sleep in the middle of the night or just before the alarm clock goes off in the morning. This is when solutions hit you that you otherwise would not come up with. Fortunately, it is not hard to try to remember these thoughts when they come in the night, at times to great benefit. Many people learn to deliberately use this phenomenon to deal with problems, rather than fight them during the day. It is amazing how many solutions to puzzles of the types we deal with in making models come easily at these times. It seems that there really is something to the phrase "let's sleep on it."

Chapter 4
The Three Stages of Model Making

When we discuss model making with people, many have difficulty imagining how models, especially scratch built ones, are made at all. On further discussion, they may be able to conceptualize the physical assembly of parts of the model, but not where the parts came from. There is much more to making a model than putting its parts together.

Making scratch-built models is done in a series of stages, each as important as the other. It is important to understand the sequence and reason for each of these stages.

Stage 1. Research

The first stage is research, which includes deciding on your subject, determining what information is needed and locating and acquiring as much of that information as you can in order to make plans to work from and to answer any and all pertinent questions that may come up about the boat.

Over time, you will learn to truly "see" the subject boat. By this I mean developing a thorough understanding of it, not only insofar as knowing what it's called when you see it, but to be able to comprehend its shapes, to be able to accurately and thoroughly recognize its various characteristics and, after some experience, to understand why it is designed in the way that it is. This last point is based on the principle that there is reasoning behind every boat's design. For the most part, the things that are similar among boats, the things that make them different from one another, are deliberately planned. The reasons for these differences in design have to do with what the boat has to do and under what conditions. We will be discussing a lot of these points as we delve further into the characteristics of boats and especially when we discuss why a Chesapeake Deadrise is designed the way that it is.

The usual types of information you would try to gather include photographs, lines drawings (See Chapter 16), historical information, and written information such as dimensions. Generally when we discuss photographs, we are talking about shots that you take yourself, but others may also be found in books, magazines, and boat catalogs. Usable photographs should be of the boat as a whole, as well as of any and all areas and parts that will be represented in your model.

Lines drawings are often, but not always, available, especially for newer styles of boats. We will discuss lines drawings in detail, with emphasis on how to read them and how to draw simple ones of your own. The amount of written information available can vary greatly, depending upon the boat. Common sources for all types of information include public libraries, maritime museums, and on the Internet.

Figure 1. During research, we want any and all photos that we can get of the subject boat. We will use the *Annie Buck* as an example. This is a shot from the starboard quarter. It is not easy to get shots without other items in them. These items are actually beneficial, because they can provide size and other references for understanding the boat better. *Courtesy of David and Ann Phillips.*

Figure 2. Another shot of the *Annie Buck*: This time it is a direct shot at the bow. *Courtesy of David and Ann Phillips.*

Figure 3. The most useful shot, if there are thoughts of tracing the boat's outline, is a moderately distant "broadside." If it can be taken right from the center of the boat, it is the view that has the least distortion. *Courtesy of David and Ann Phillips.*

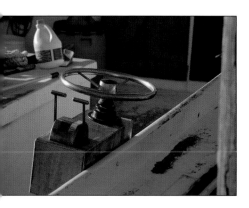

Figure 4. It is important to take photographs of any and all features that you want to put into your model. This is especially true for interior features, such as walls, bulkheads, motor boxes, and flooring. Any hardware or other detailed features, such as this steering pedestal, should have their own images. *Courtesy of David and Ann Phillips.*

Figure 5. It is always good to see if there are any marine drawings available for the boat you choose. If they were made by the original designer, or you know that they are accurate, your model is more likely to be, as well. It will also save you a lot of effort, because you won't have to figure out the measurements yourself.

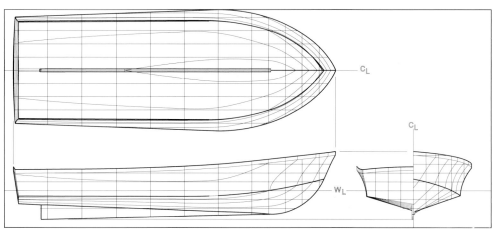

You can never have too much information about a boat, but you can have too little. It would not be the end of the world, but if your subject boat is no longer available and you get close to the end of making your model only to discover that you don't know what something looked like, you may have to interpolate, which means to fill in the blanks, based on a best guess estimation. This can easily happen, even with something as substantial as the top of a cabin roof, because it is often out of view when you take photos. It's good, when looking at a boat, or at your assembled information, to ask yourself if there is anything that you can't see that might be important later on.

By the same token, information on a vessel that is long gone may be essentially nonexistent. In such cases, there may be only one photo, or an old painting of the subject boat. In this case you have no choice but to fill in information, based upon what you've got. Again, understanding why boats are designed in the ways they are helps you to know what would and would not make sense. Additionally, finding out information about boats that had the same purpose, from the same area and from the same era can be very helpful in determining the probability of other features being present or not.

The overall results of your research should be that you have acquired the best available information and that it is ready to use it for the design of your model.

Figure 6. When people ask us what photos to take in order for us to make a model of their boat, we tell them to imagine holding a model of their boat, in their hand, and to notice everything that they can see. Take photos of all of those things. Then imagine all of the things that you can't see. Take photos of those things, too. Try not to leave anything out. While a relatively simple concept, it usually leads to a good set of pictures to work from.

Stage 2. Planning

The second stage is planning. In the planning stage, the objective is to make plans for construction and determine what materials and tools will be required. Here is where you choose how you will approach your model: what size, what type of construction, how much detail, and how you want to display it. Your abilities and resources will have to be taken into account in your planning.

The drawings that we work with in the research stage differ from those that develop during the planning stage, in that they are of the subject boat itself. Since a model is not exactly the same thing as the original boat, drawings in the planning stage should be drawings of the model.

Planning may mean that you use your own mechanical drawings or drawings made by others. There is no requirement that your drawings and notes conform to other people's standards, as long as they work for you. That you understand the information in them is what is important. The more accurate your drawings, the better your model will be. It's the same as with research. The more complete and accurate your research is, the better your planning can be.

If, in your research, you are able to get good marine drawings, you can take them to a specialty printing shop and have them scaled to the size you will be working at, as many model makers we know have done. In this case, you can work directly from those drawings and add your own notes where needed.

Figure 8. One thing that made this model work was to design plans for it to be a model and not the original boat. The viewer should see the boat; the builder should see the model. If you look closely, many things that make it look real are actually different from their counterparts on the real boat. We are often using the power of suggestion.

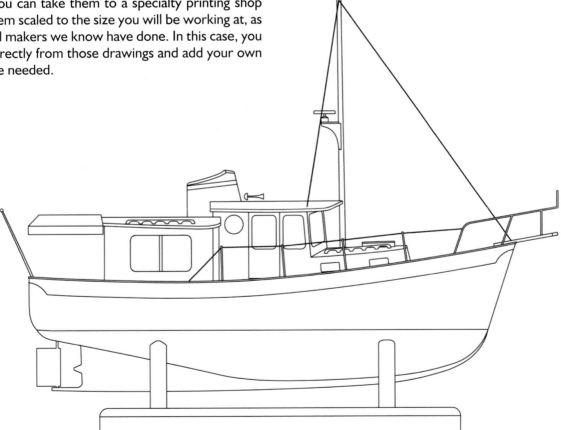

Figure 7. Although it may not seem to make common sense, at first, you will get better results in your planning when you conceptualize what you are making as a model, as opposed to a miniature of the real boat.

Planning is the stage where you are initially faced with the puzzles that we mentioned before:

- What size?
- What style?
- What construction method?

As you answer each of these questions, things start to fall into place and you begin to get a good sense of what you need to start doing. It's as if a pathway becomes visible. Once you decide that you want your model to have a certain style, you will see that one type of construction may be better than another, which answers the question of which construction method to use. Once you decide to use a certain type of construction, then you know that you have to design things in the way that this type of construction requires. This design requirement provides the answers to questions of materials and tools and the sequence of answers, like a line of falling Dominoes, changes the previously formidable fog known as "where do I start" into a clear sequence of things that need to be done.

There may be a few things that cannot be fully planned until you are actually building your model. Because of the nature of model making, some really good things come from experimentation and it may not be until you are in the shop that you can work out final answers, but the vast majority of what you will be doing should be settled while you are planning.

Figure 9. The planning stage is when you need to decide what style of model you want to make, such as this half-hull. This decision leads to answers of other questions, because different methods of construction work better for different styles of presentation. Half hulls are often made by the "lift-building" method. This is the *American Eagle*, an America's Cup contender made by Grover Into.

Figure 10. The *Oldsquaw* is a Chesapeake Bay Draketail and is built from the "split-hull" method. The split-hull method is relatively easy to learn and can be used for simple or highly complex models. This is a waterline model, but the method also works well for full-hulled models.

Figure 11. This 1964 Century Coronado was built using the "plank on bulkhead" method of construction. Plank on bulkhead construction requires more planning than the previous methods. Models of this detail can take years to make. *Courtesy of Robert Green Jr.*

The results of planning should be that you have made a reasonable design, you have made all of the necessary decisions to begin building your model, and that you have assembled the resources to begin construction. Planning well will mean that you don't have any surprises when you construct your model. In certain ways, the result of good planning is akin to having created a model boat kit for yourself.

Figure 12. What is it and how am I going to make something that looks like it? This puzzle may or may not be fully settled before construction starts.

Stage 3: Construction

The third stage is construction. This is the stage that most people can already partially envision. The questions of how do I proceed will pretty much have been answered during the planning process. The construction stage is where your raw materials are worked to conform to your plans. It is where all cutting, assembly, making of detail parts, painting, and all other physical techniques are done. As with the other stages, the better research and planning that you do, the easier construction will be. It should be a matter of following the instructions that you made for yourself in the planning stage.

Even when you are building from a kit, understanding these stages and applying them to your project will improve your results. Applying a research stage means getting to know as much about your subject as possible. It is not unusual to come across something on a boat that is unfamiliar. It is much better to get to know what that object is beforehand than to guess. Sometimes kit makers alter the design from the original to the model, in order to make the kit easier to build. Things that frequently vary from real boats to kits include: widths and numbers of deck planks, hardware, and paint schemes. A small amount of research gives you the ability to modify and/or correct these issues and create a far more realistic model.

Likewise, planning means checking to make sure that your kit has all of the parts that it should (especially if the kit is an antique), that you will be able to understand the directions and that you have all of the tools, glues, pins, clothespins, and other things necessary in advance.

As with scratch-building, the construction stage should just be a matter of following the original instructions along with any others that you have added.

Again: Research – Planning – Construction.

Organizing your project in this way will help demystify the overall process and give you a sense of control over how the end product comes out.

This whole book contains information that will give you the knowledge to accomplish all three stages. Now, let's spend some time with boats...

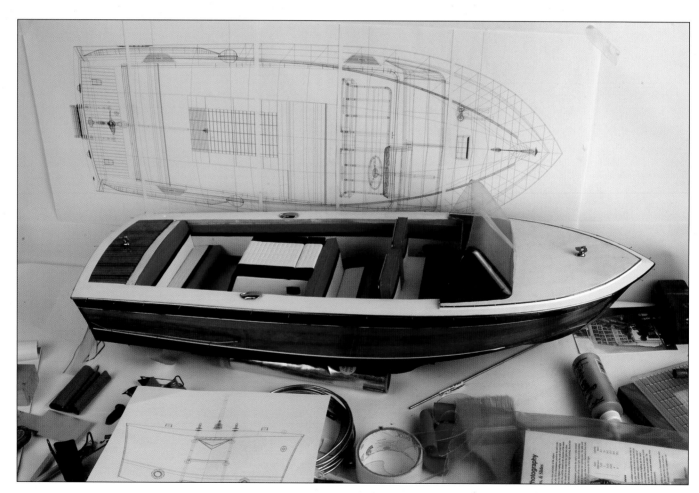

Figure 13. This photo of the model in Figure 11 was taken during its construction stage. Tools on the table were used to make and assemble the various parts that we designed in the planning stage as per our drawings. The information needed to create the drawing came from our work in the research stage.

Chapter 5
The Structural Elements of Boats

Learning to identify a boat is a matter of learning to differentiate the features it has relative to other boats. We can break the major structural elements of boats into five categories: hull, deck, superstructure, type of power, and other gear. Secondarily, we can also look at construction methods and materials, colors, sizes, and overall style of combined features. This last point refers to how to know the difference between a Ferryboat and a Fishing boat, by being able to compare their respective features.

Figure 1. An automobile ferry: This particular boat is guided by a cable that runs from riverbank to riverbank. Its power system must work in two directions. Many ferries have propellers at each end. It must align with ramps at each end, which may involve extra equipment on the boat and on land.

Figure 2. New England fishing boats: These vessels have very high
and sturdy bows for confronting potentially heavy seas in the ocean.

Figure 3. A
rendezvous of
sailing vessels: If
you look closely,
you will see that
at least three of
them are virtually
identical.

Every boat has a **hull:** The hull of a boat can be thought of as similar to the foundation of a house or the chassis of a car. It is the body upon which the rest of the boat is built. It is the "vessel" that allows it to float. Some boats are virtually nothing but hull.

Figure 4. A boat version that is purely hull: This boat, which is about 5 feet long, is used by its Captain to ferry to his workboat, which is kept at a mooring, a permanent anchor, out in the water, away from land.

Examples of boats that are mainly hull include canoes, rowboats, and barges. All hulls can be classified as displacement, planing or a combination of the two. Displacement hulls ride deep in the water, while planing hulls lift out of the water at higher speeds, reducing friction and increasing economy. Some boats have more than one hull, as in the case of catamarans (two hulls) and trimarans (three hulls). Sailboat hulls, with their deep keels, tend to have greater draft than similarly sized powerboats.

Figure 6. A Chincoteague Scow: a very efficient and sturdy planing hull design.

Figure 5. An excellent view of a sailboat's displacement hull: Note the ballasted keel at the bottom, which is essential to the boat's operation when underway and for its overall stability. Note also the increase in water depth required compared to the planing hull boat in Figure 6.

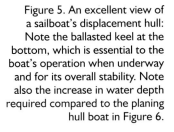

The **deck:** The deck is at the top of the hull. It encloses the hull so that water doesn't ride up over the hull's top edge and, in most cases, provides a surface to walk upon. Decks are usually "crowned," which means arched, so that water runs off of them and back into the water rather than pooling, which can cause damage. Almost all boats have crowning that runs from side to side, but on many boats it also runs from bow to stern. Thus the shape of many decks is mildly convex.

Superstructure: Almost all larger boats and ships have some type of **superstructure.** Superstructure refers to physical structural features of the boat that are above the deck and can include pilothouses, living quarters, bridges, and other things that are integral to the boat itself. A tugboat has a noticeably different superstructure than a cabin cruiser. Superstructure does not refer to the masts, booms or other items that would come under the heading of running gear for sailing vessels. Other large items above the deck may fall under the category of other gear as seen in figure 9.

Figure 7. The elegant planked deck of a mahogany and chrome classic boat. Note the crowning of the deck.

Figure 9. On this ship the rear housing structure and exhaust stack would be considered superstructure in our categorization. Forward of that are four cranes, which would fall under the category of other gear. Such a ship is called a "self-loader." Ships of this type are able to go to ports that do not have their own cranes, giving them access to ports that other ships cannot use. Note that the bow is higher than the stern, indicating that there is more cargo in the rear of the ship. Also notice the bulbous bow breaking the water.

Figure 8. This portion of deck presents a whole different set of colors, textures, and objects. The type of cabin shown here is called a "trunk cabin." A trunk cabin rises above the surface of the main deck and is surrounded by a walkway. The surface of this deck is fiberglass with non-skid texturing to prevent slipping when wet. *Courtesy of Michael B. Finegan.*

Figure 10. The superstructure of the *Annie Buck* consists of the pilot-house and cabin, again a trunk cabin. *Courtesy of David and Ann Phillips.*

Running gear: The equipment that causes a boat to move and to control that movement. For sailing vessels, it refers to sails, masts, booms, rigging, and other equipment involved in the movement of the boat. For a powerboat it includes rudder, propeller, prop-shaft, prop struts, outboard motors, out-drives, and other motive elements. When a powerboat is in the water, the running gear is usually hidden from view.

Other gear: Depending upon the boat, there will be other accessories that are essential to it and others representative of its type. We are referring to those things that are not physically part of the boat's original structure, but help define the type of boat that it is, because the boat's function is dependent upon their presence. For instance, deep sea fishing boats will generally have outriggers. Shrimp boats will have large winches, nets, and derricks. Crab boats will have winders and oyster boats will have culling boards, which are used to sort the oysters by size and quality.

Other examples of gear that would define the purpose of the boat could be such items as tow rings on ski boats, or radar equipment on boats that go out to sea.

Figure 11. The running gear of this sailboat consists of mast, boom, sails, steering system, auxiliary engine, and many lines and pieces of hardware. Here are just a few of those lines. *Courtesy of Michael B. Finegan.*

Figure 13. Winders, which are line-handling devices, are used extensively on boats that harvest seafood. This type is used for "trot lining," a method of crabbing. This one belongs to the *Annie Buck. Courtesy of David and Ann Phillips.*

Figure 12. This small outboard with a combination steering/throttle lever is all the running gear needed for a small aluminum fishing boat.

Figure 14. The boat on the left has a mast and boom. This mast and boom have nothing to do with sailing. These are part of the system used to tow and haul in the oyster dredge, the mesh object in the center of the boat. Both boats are versions of deadrises.

Figure 15. A boat configured for soft clamming. Two derricks are holding up a hydraulic rig that carries the clams up from the seabed. This type of hull is often referred to as a sea sled. Note the aft pilothouse.

Chapter 6
Making a Paper Model

A model from paper? Are we kidding? Not at all. Paper is used to make models all the time, especially architectural models. Paper is a very useful material in many aspects of model making. It is much easier to make box-shaped objects with paper than it is to make boats, but it can be done, as you are about to see. If anyone gives you a hard time about making a paper model, tell them that it's your "developable surfaces" model.

With paper and other flexible panel materials, such as very thin plywood, you can bend shapes such as tubes, cones, and simple curves. You cannot bend paper in more than one direction at a time, though, or it will crumble or rip. Shapes that can be made with paper, because they are only curved in one direction, are referred to as developable surfaces and this is an extremely important concept in the design of boats.

We'll be discussing curvature in much greater depth in some of the following chapters, but note that any bends of the paper in this model can only occur in a single direction.

This is not a scratch-built model. It's really more of a kit. The main reason for making this model is so you can get started with handling a 3-dimensional version of our subject boat and so you have a reference tool that you can look at when we discuss the various terminology and theories we will be talking about throughout the book.

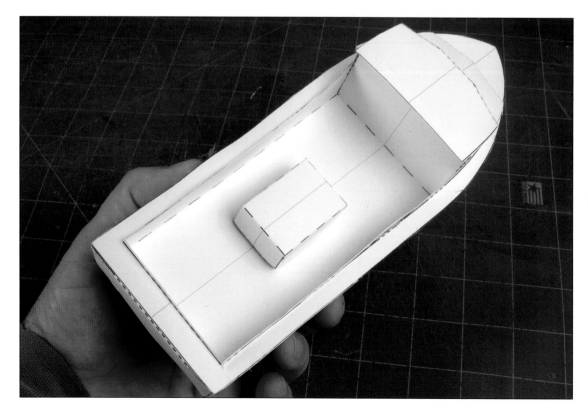

Figure 1. A paper model of a Chesapeake Deadrise boat.

You will need to use a copy machine (don't cut from the book, please) or scanner and printer in order to print copies of the plans. Printing them at 100% will give a one quarter inch to the foot model (.25":1' scale). Regular weight paper is usable, but heavier stock is both easier to work with and more durable. It is made from paper, after all. Personally, I would probably make two or three copies, in case anything gets damaged.

For cutting, you can use scissors, although I prefer to use a hobby knife and cutting mat. You can hold things together with cellophane tape, or high tack glue, which I believe results in a better-looking model. I would also rec-ommend having a thin straightedge, such as a metal ruler, to help make your bends crisp.

Once you have your tools and materials, it shouldn't take more than a few hours to make this model. I am not going to give you detailed step by step directions, since you are learning to become a scratch builder and I want you to have to think about the construction process as you go along. If there are any puzzles here, they won't be hard to solve. As you proceed, you might be able to envision some improvements to my design. That said, the instructions that I give you should be adequate to **get** you through without any problems.

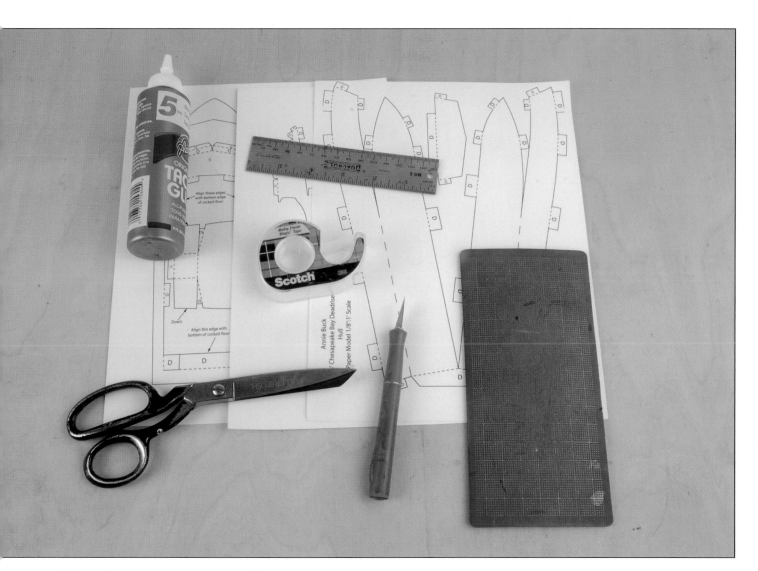

Figure 2. You don't need a lot of tools to make this model.

Plans

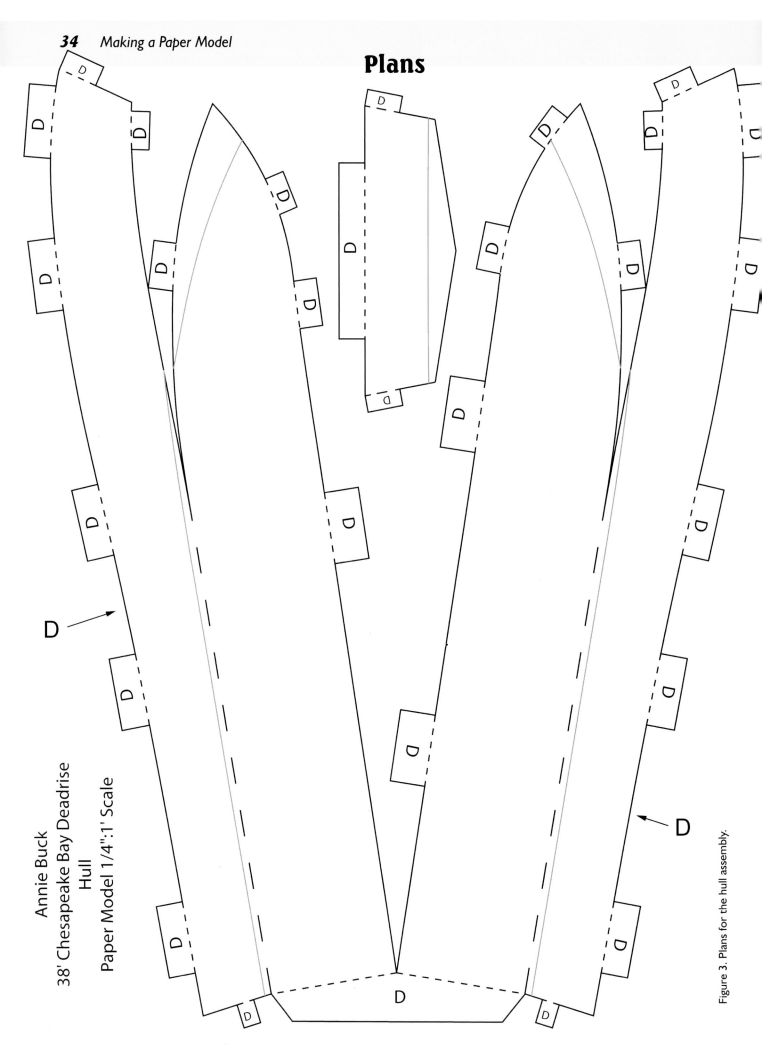

Annie Buck
38' Chesapeake Bay Deadrise
Hull
Paper Model 1/4":1' Scale

Figure 3. Plans for the hull assembly.

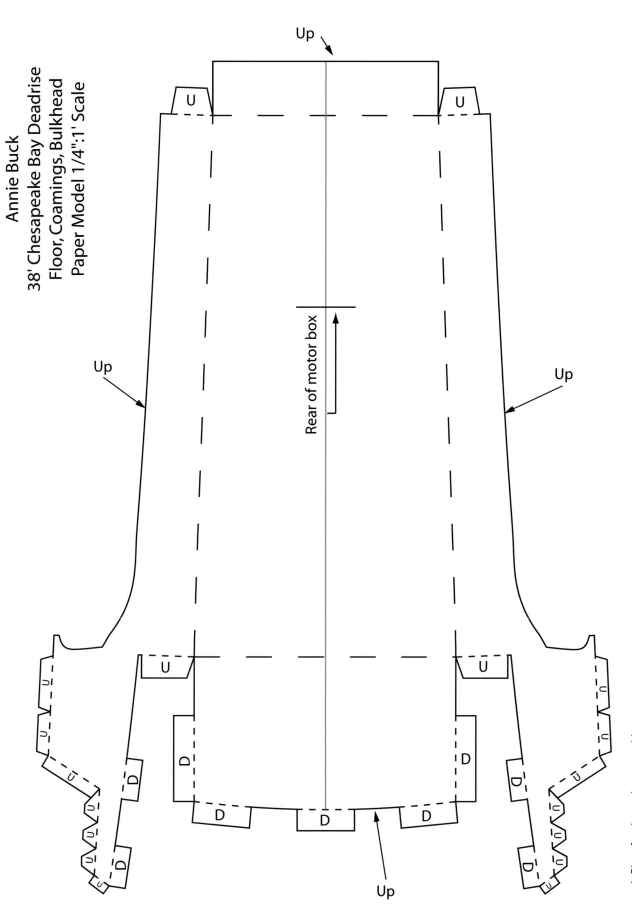

Annie Buck
38' Chesapeake Bay Deadrise
Floor, Coamings, Bulkhead
Paper Model 1/4":1' Scale

Up

U

U

Up

Up

Rear of motor box

U

U

D

D

D

D

D

Up

Figure 4. Plans for the cockpit assembly.

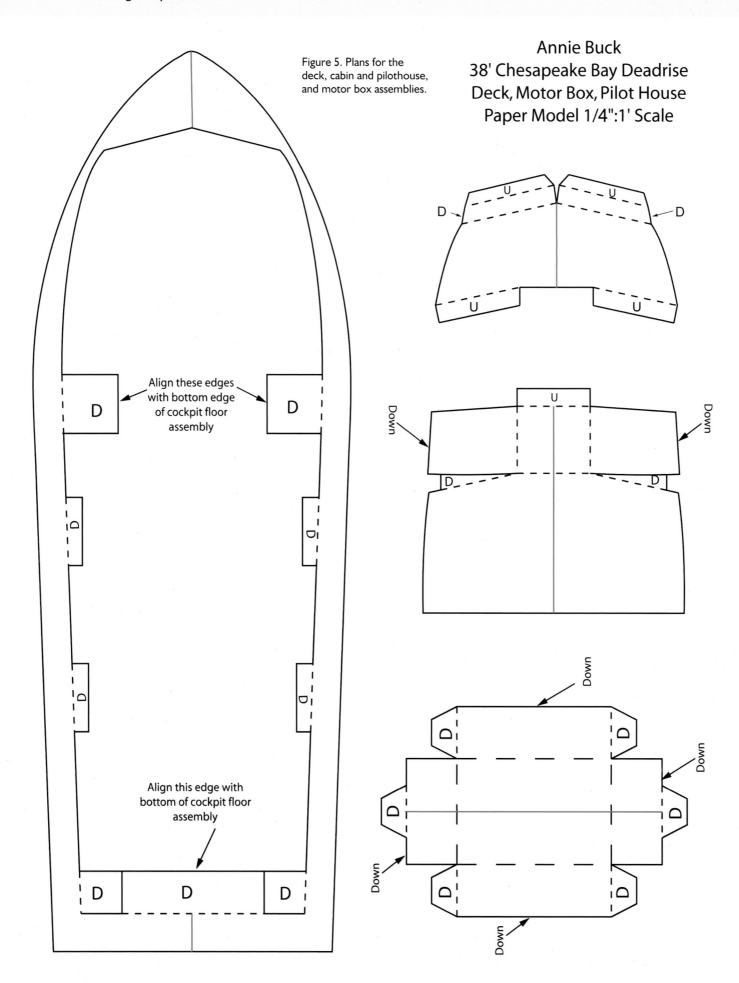

Figure 5. Plans for the deck, cabin and pilothouse, and motor box assemblies.

**Annie Buck
38' Chesapeake Bay Deadrise
Deck, Motor Box, Pilot House
Paper Model 1/4":1' Scale**

Align these edges with bottom edge of cockpit floor assembly

Align this edge with bottom of cockpit floor assembly

Annie Buck
38' Chesapeake Bay Deadrise
Windows and Skeg
Paper Model 1/4":1' Scale

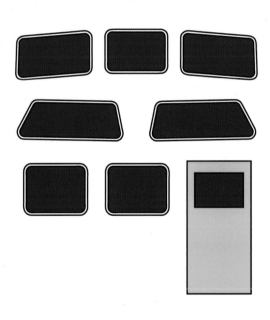

Figure 6. Plans for optional items, including windows and skeg.

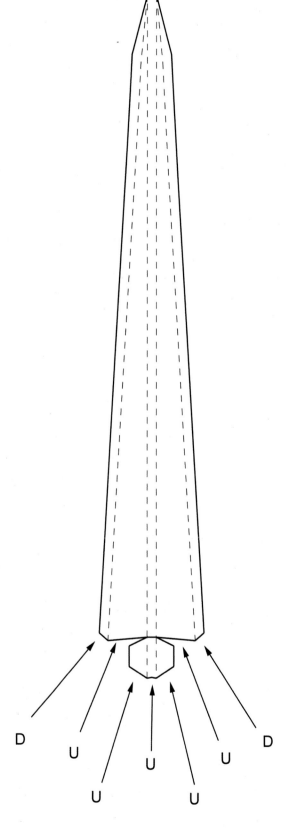

Instructions

Cut all solid black lines. Do not cut any colored lines. Do not cut any dashed lines. Note that there are written instructions that will remain with your waste paper, so don't throw it away. You'll need to know how to find these instructions when your pieces are cut out. This is another good reason for making extra copies.

The model is composed of panels with tabs for attaching them to each other. Each tab is labeled "U" or "D". If you are looking down at your paper, a "U" means to bend upward and a "D" means to bend downward. Likewise, there are up and down notations on your waste material. They refer to larger areas to be bent as a whole and most of the bends that they refer to are marked with larger dashes. Some bends are meant to be harder than others; don't bend things too hard.

All bends are along straight lines, even though they may not appear to be. This means that a straightedge can be used to help make any of your creases. It is very important that you do not make a crease anywhere that isn't marked, or that part might be ruined. When everything comes together, there are gentle curves in many areas that won't look right if they have creases in them and, more importantly, such creases could compromise the rigidity of the model. When assembled properly, all tabs should be within the model's structure where you can't see them.

I recommend that you start with the hull assembly. I would make the smaller creases for the tabs first and then make the longer ones. Do not try to get the hull to come together until you are certain that all of your creases are made or you may put too much stress on the main panels. The first attachments to be made are right in the middle working from the back of the boat toward the front. Make sure that all edges meet as closely and cleanly as possible. All tabs should end up on the inside of the hull. If gluing, make sure you give the glue a moment to set. One or two minutes are really all you need.

As you work forward, you will notice that the hull wants to assume its proper shape. Let it. This is the way that developable surfaces come together. Continue attaching the tabs to the parts of the panels that they naturally go to until you have your hull shaped. The transom is basically a cap that attaches to the rear of the assembly that you just made. You are finished with the hull assembly when the only remaining tabs are along the top edges.

Figure 7. Working from the rear to bring the hull assembly together.

The next sub-assembly should be the floor, coamings, and bulkhead. Again, make creases for the small tabs first. Be careful to make your longer creases right down the middles of the dashed lines. When folded together, the assembly should resemble a box.

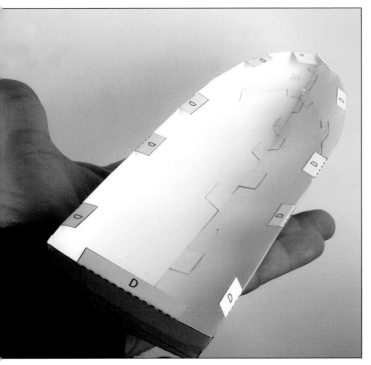

Figure 8. The completed hull assembly.

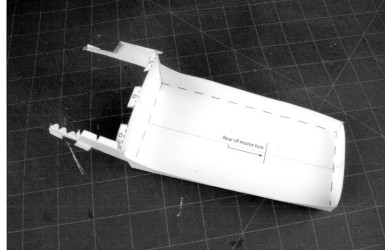

Figure 10. The completed cockpit assembly.

One of the trickiest parts of the model is the connection of the deck to the cockpit assembly. Note that the long tabs must go to the bottom of the cockpit box to be in the right location.

Figure 9. Using a metal ruler as a straightedge for making sharp creases on the cockpit assembly.

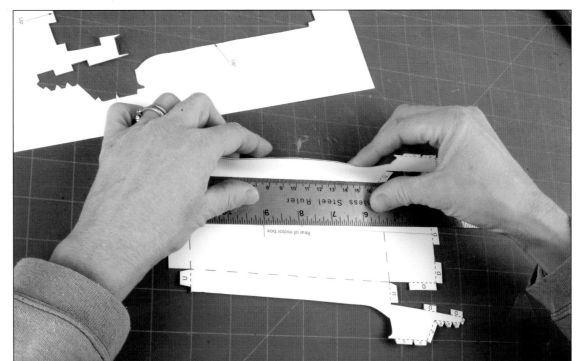

I recommend that when you attach the deck to the hull, you fit things together at the bow area first. It is possible that you will have to loosen and adjust something that you did earlier to make it all come together.

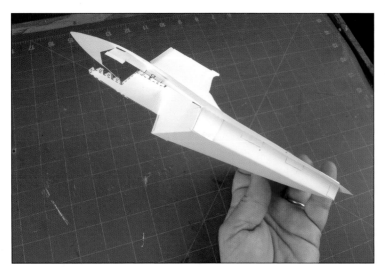

Figure 11. How the forward deck forward tabs should fit with the cockpit assembly. Note that the rear tabs also run to the bottom of the cockpit box. This leaves part of the coaming to protrude above the deck.

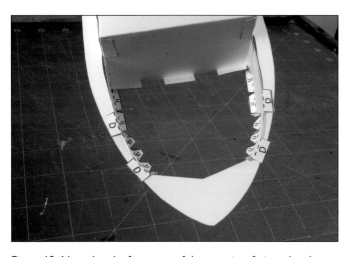

Figure 12. Note that the front part of the coamings fit in and under the foredeck. This view is from underneath the bow.

Figure 13. The trick to making the pilot-house/cabin assembly work is to fit them together like this.

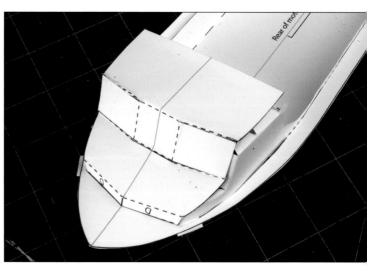

Figure 14. How the cabin/pilothouse assembly should look before gluing to the cockpit assembly.

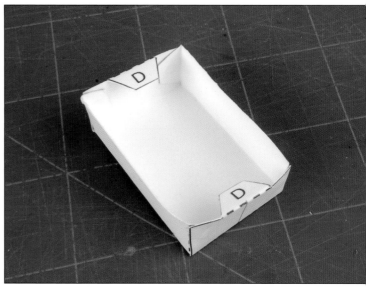

Figure 15. The assembled motor box from underneath.

The fact that this model is made of paper is good and bad. It's bad, because it's not very durable and you have to be careful with it. It's good because it's not hard to make and you can always make another one. Each time you do it, and I know this from experience, it comes out much better than the one before it.

The other good thing about it being made from paper is that you can write on it, if you want. We are going to be discussing a lot of concepts and terms and one way to keep notes is on your boat. You will also be surprised at how much you can dress a model like this one up. If you add graphics and other "things" that are found on a boat, you will find that it starts to look more and more like the real thing.

Let's start into some new concepts. Keep your new boat handy for reference.

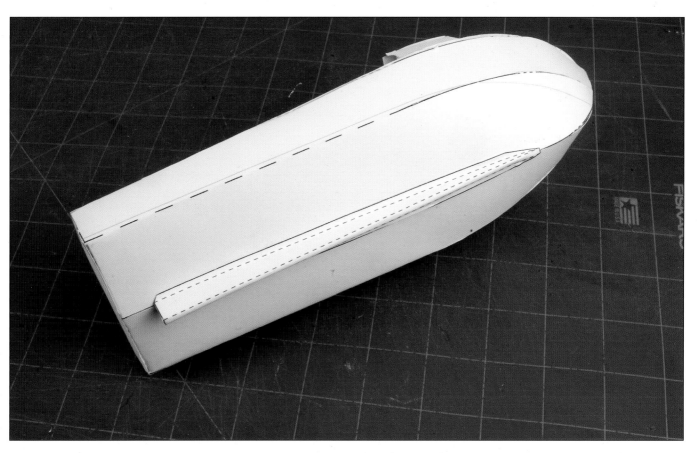

Figure 16. If you choose to make the skeg, it should look like this when finished.

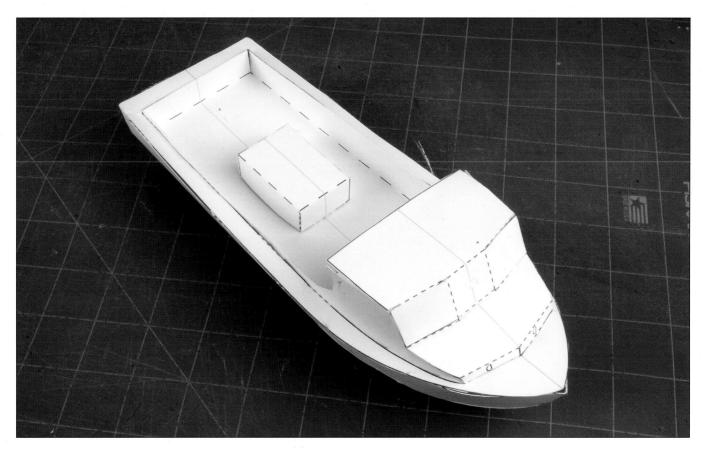

Figure 17. It may not be elegant, but it is a model and you just made it.

Chapter 7
Descriptive Features of Boat Hulls

There is a lot of terminology regarding boats and the maritime world that can be hard to keep straight unless you spend a lot of time around boats and frequently use the language. There are lots and lots of odd sounding nautical terms used to describe anything and everything that one finds in and around boats. The fact of the matter is that the maritime world is very specialized in a way that can be compared to the way any industry, or way of life, such as the aviation world, or the computer-programming world, would be specialized. Add to this fact that the maritime way of life is among the oldest there is and the lexicon becomes amazingly large.

As with other specialized fields, the maritime world has developed words that only pertain to maritime things. In the same way that it would be hard to tune up a car without knowing what a spark plug is, it is hard to conceptualize the shape of a boat if every part of it is referred to as a "whatchamacallit". Even though nautical words may seem strange, in many cases unwieldy, they are words that you can use to converse with others who understand boats and it's so much better to learn them than to make up your own. The terms that we are primarily concerned with, as model makers, describe boat parts, measurement, and spatial concepts, as well as designations of areas in and around boats.

The dominant part of a boat is its hull. Compared to all other aspects of a boat, it is the largest single factor in determining a boat's performance and capability. It is what the rest of the boat is built upon. In most cases it is also the single most complex part of the boat, both dimensionally and structurally. Figure 1 shows the primary lines that define a boat's hull.

All boats have a **bow**, which is the front end and a **stern**, which is the rear end. Almost all boats have a **keel**, although it is not always clearly defined. The keel is essentially the backbone of the boat and runs along the center of the bottom of the hull. In fact, in wooden boats, the keel is often the first part or assembly built. Although a seldom used practice today, some boat builders, whose work was not done from printed plans, would build the keel to a length which was determined by the size and amount of wood they could get. They would then calculate the dimensions of all other parts of the boat using formulas factored upon the keel's length. For example, the widest part of the hull would be a certain percentage of the length of the keel. In such construction, the keel can be very important in determining the size of the boat.

The **sheerline** is the top edge of the hull's sides and is most often, but not always, higher at the bow end than the stern end. Both the sheerline and the chines help define the shape of the hull in a drawing when seen from the front or top views. Looking at the top view of Figure 1, you can see that, for this entire boat, the sheerline comprises the outermost dimensions. This is usually the case, but there are exceptions as in the case of tumblehome, which we will discuss shortly.

The **transom** is the wide and more or less flat rear face of the boat. It is currently the most common type of stern structure; however, it is only one of many styles. It is easy to picture the image of a canoe, in which it could be said that there are two bows and no stern. There are some larger workboats that have what appears to be a bow shape at each end, referred to as "double-enders." They are more common in waters where there is significant surf activity. Modern fiberglass boats often have molded-in swim platforms, rather than transoms.

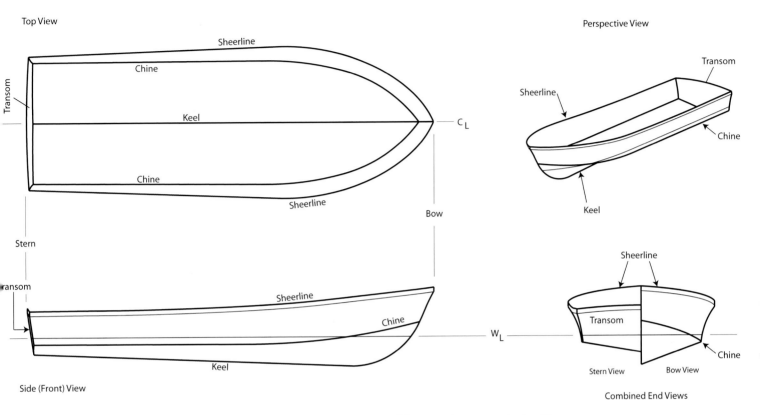

Top View

Sheerline

Chine

Transom

Keel

Chine

Sheerline

C_L

Bow

Stern

Transom

Sheerline

Chine

Keel

Side (Front) View

Perspective View

Transom

Sheerline

Chine

Keel

Sheerline

Transom

Chine

W_L

Stern View   Bow View

Combined End Views

Figure 1. Shows a generic representation of the most common hull shape used for powerboats over the last 50 years. Any boat with this type of hull, no matter what its dimensions are, has the attributes shown here.

The **chines** are the edges at the bottoms of the hull's sides, as well as, the outer edges of the hull's bottom. Its shape and position is not always distinct. In many boats, the transition from bottom to sides is rounded. This is extremely significant. Hulls with "hard chines," as shown in figure 3, generally belong to **planing hulls**, while those with "soft chines" or "rounded bilges" are found on **displacement hulls**.

Canoe

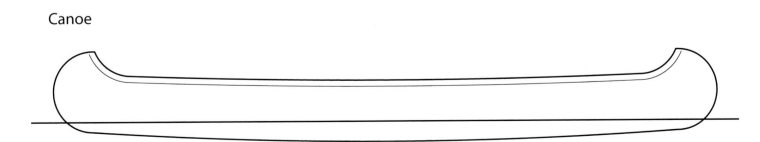

Figure 2: A canoe can be thought of as having two bows and no transom.

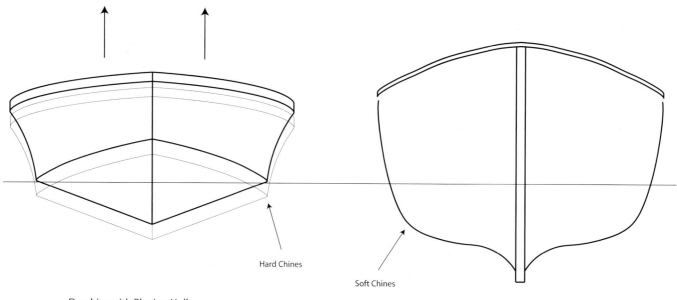

Hard Chines

Soft Chines

Deadrise with Planing Hull

Pleasure Trawler with Displacement Hull

Figure 3. The difference between hard and soft chines and how they provide visual clues to differentiate planing vs. displacement hulls. At higher speeds, planing hulls lift out of the water as shown by the heavier lines on the left hull. Displacement hulls, which don't, run deeper and are less affected by water surface conditions.

Planing hulls change their performance characteristics when the boat reaches a certain rate of speed. At that threshold, the hull "lifts" out of the water, riding on top of it, reducing the amount of surface area that makes contact with the water so that drag is significantly reduced and allowing for much higher speed and efficiency. The chines do not cause the lifting affect, which is created by the larger, flatter surfaces on the bottom of the hull. They are, however, a recognizable characteristic of virtually all planing hulls.

Figure 4. This boat has reached planing speed and is traveling on top of the water in a way that is similar to skimming a flat rock over the surface of water.

Displacement hulls do not lift out of the water and tend to run at slower speeds. They can handle rougher seas than planing hulls, because, riding deeper in the water, the activity of the water's surface has less overall effect on them. Some boats combine the benefits of both and have what are called semi-displacement hulls. There are many variations of chine arrangements including multiple chines, flat chines, reverse chines and others, however for purposes of description, we will focus on hard and soft. When it comes time to learn these distinctions, you will understand their shapes without our help.

You should now be able, when looking at illustrations, to identify the Bow, Stern, Transom, Sheerline, Chines, and Keel of most boats.

Figures 5 through 8 show images of two boats of the same length. The *Annie Buck* is a 38' Chesapeake deadrise, a powered workboat that has a planing hull. The *Gratitude* is a 38' cruising sailboat with a displacement hull. Note that the features we have discussed in this chapter are present on both. Although you cannot see either boat's features beneath the waterline, in the next four photographs, what you can see of the sheerline and other features reveals strong contrasts in design elements which are hallmarks of each boat's respective purpose.

Figure 5. The *Annie Buck* from the starboard bow.
Courtesy of David and Ann Phillips.

Figure 7. The *Gratitude* from a bit forward of port broadside.
Courtesy of Michael B. Finegan.

Figure 6. The *Annie Buck* from the port stern.
Courtesy of David and Ann Phillips.

Figure 8. The *Gratitude* from the port stern: If you could see below the waterline of *Gratitude*, you would see a strong similarity to the hull in Figure 5, in Chapter 5. *Courtesy of Michael B. Finegan.*

As you can see, there are significant distinctions between the two types of hull, even without seeing the parts of them that are below the waterline. Often times, you will not be able to see a boat's underwater features, but even so, it is usually possible to distinguish planing from displacement hulls.

The occasions when it is possible to see below the waterlines of larger boats occur when they are "hauled out," which is to say removed from the water for maintenance or storage. Such opportunities for seeing boat hulls in their entirety should be considered lucky and are certainly to be taken advantage of when possible.

Due to the darkness of the building where *Gratitude* was being stored, we were unable to get really high quality photographs, but there should be enough information to see that her rounded hull does not have distinct chines. Compare the similarity of her shape to that of the sailboat in Figure 5 of Chapter 5.

We were lucky enough to get some photos of the *Annie Buck*, when she was hauled out for routine maintenance. You can clearly see the shapes of the chines and the keel. Note that the chines are visible above the waterline in the bow area, which is true for the vast majority of planing hull boats and is a good clue to look for when trying to determine what lies below.

Before we leave the subject of features that comprise boat hulls, we need to discuss two terms that are extremely important to boat design.

The first is **flare**. The vast majority of boats have flare, especially in the bow area. A section of a boat that is flared is one where the sheerline is wider than the chine line. When viewed from the front of a boat, flare appears as a "V" shape. There are a number of reasons for flare in the bow of a boat. It allows for a wide and more spacious foredeck and a hull that can be narrow and streamlined at the waterline. It also causes water to be forced aside, helping to keep the upper parts of the boat dry, especially when moving through choppy waters.

In Figure 10, you can see that "Annie Buck" has a healthy amount of bow flare. If you've noticed a difference between the appearance of the flare of your model and the appearance of the flare in Figure 10, it means you are using good observational skills. This pertains to the difference between the developable, or single curved, surfaces that make up your model and the compound curved surfaces of the actual boat. We will discuss compound curves in detail later in this book.

Figure 9. The hull of *Gratitude* is rounded from sheer line to keel through much of her length (note the curvature of the ropes). The distance between her hull and those of neighboring hulls is merely inches. This is a very elegant and classic hull design. *Courtesy of Michael B. Finegan.*

Figure 10. The chine and keel are clearly visible in this shot of the *Annie Buck*. Note how high the chine line rises above the waterline. The cradle that supports the hull rides on railroad tracks, which are inclined in such a way that as the cradle is pulled, it and the boat that it supports lift clear of the water. This mechanism is referred to as a marine railway and is a means used to haul out large boats and small ships in boatyards throughout the world. *Courtesy of David and Ann Phillips.*

Sportfishing boats are particularly well known for their flared bows, because they are used in coastal ocean waters, where conditions can become quite rough. Note how flare differs from one boat to another, as in the line of sportfishers shown in Figure 11.

Figure 11. One of the best places to see flare is on sport fishing boats such as these. Flare basically means that the width of the sheer line is wider than the width of the chines at a given section. All have flared bows, but each has its own variations.

The second concept we want to mention is **tumblehome.** Tumblehome is the opposite of flare and is usually found at the stern of the boat. It is when the sides of the boat move upward and inward from the chines to the sheerline. Again, it is a feature that results in a drier ride for some boats. It is found more often on older wooden boats.

Flare and tumblehome are good examples of features that can make a boat's shape complex. Both came about as the result of the constant search, by designers, for ways to make boats function better. Variations of flare and tumblehome have also become key stylistic elements. You have probably seen boats that, for some reason, really seem to have perfect lines. A boat's beauty usually lies in its curves. Often, the really beautiful boats have more complex curves in its surfaces.

The Difference Between Single and Compound Curved Surfaces

Boats are notorious for having surfaces with "compound curves." The opposite is a single, or developable curve. Single curved surfaces are simpler to deal with. Rolling a piece of paper into a tube is to bend it on a single curve. Try to wrap that same piece of paper around a ball and it crinkles. This is because we are attempting to bend it in more than one direction at a time. Compound curved surfaces can be defined as those surfaces with contours that curve in more than one direction simultaneously. The next chapter shows how to identify features of boats that help us better understand these complex shapes.

Before we leave this chapter, I suggest that you get into the habit, when you see boats, of identifying and comparing the features that we have discussed, including the keel, sheerlines, chines, and stern construction. Also, compare the types of flare different boats have and whether or not they have tumblehome. Think about the visual differences in planing and displacement hulls. These features tell you a great deal about a boat and you will find your ability to analyze these things will become routine in no time.

Figure 12. Tumblehome, which is when the sheer line of the boat moves inboard of the waterline—usually in the boat's stern, is most common on older boats, like this mahogany classic. Many new boat builders are starting to bring the style back.

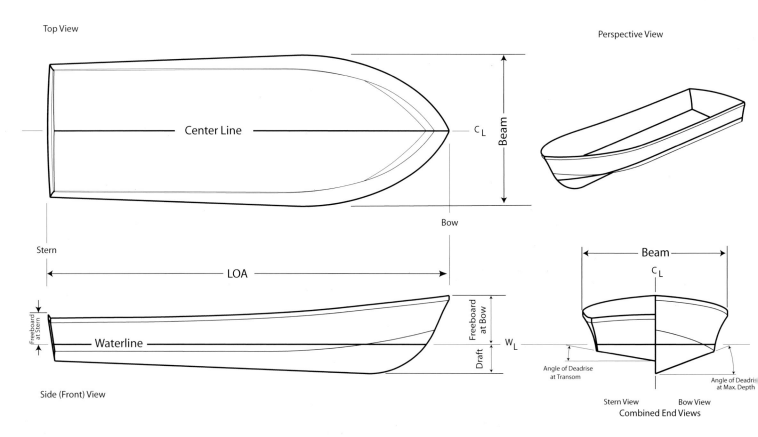

Top View

Perspective View

Center Line

C_L

Beam

Bow

Stern

LOA

Beam

C_L

Freeboard at Stern

Waterline

Freeboard at Bow

Draft

W_L

Angle of Deadrise at Transom

Angle of Deadrise at Max. Depth

Side (Front) View

Stern View

Bow View

Combined End Views

Figure 1. This 4-view drawing shows the important features of a boat's hull that are relevant for measuring purposes.

Chapter 8
Measurement Features of Boat Hulls

Boats, being what they are, can be extremely confusing when it comes to understanding measurements. The terms we refer to in this chapter include points that measurements can be made from as well as some of the most important measurements that you will need for model making purposes.

When looking at a drawings of a boat, Waterline and Centerline might be easily overlooked, but they are very important to us. They are often times seen as W sub L for Waterline and C sub L for Centerline. The line that denotes the waterline in the front view of this drawing represents the edge of a plane at the level where the surface of the water should be when the boat is put into it. More specifically, this line represents where the boat rests in the water after displacing water equal to its weight. The centerline, in the top and end views, should be thought of as the edge of a vertical plane that cuts through the exact center of the boat lengthwise.

On your paper model, a green line represents the waterline and a red line represents its centerline.

There are several ways in which these two terms are important. Most importantly, for the moment, they give us straight lines from which we can take and make measurements. Since there are very few reliable straight lines in most hulls, we need all that we can get.

Top View

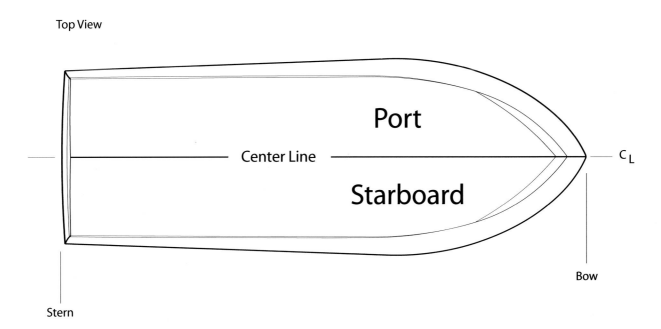

Port

Center Line — ^{C}L

Starboard

Bow

Stern

Figure 2. Sometimes the terms Port and Starboard can seem ambiguous. These are the Port and Starboard sides of a boat.

Before we proceed further, this is a good time to get something straight! The terms port and starboard can be confusing and can be used incorrectly. When you are alone, with no reference to a boat, the phrase "to your port side," is interchangeable with to your left side. The same would be true of the phrase "to your starboard side" and your right side. However, where a boat is concerned, port is the side of the boat to the left of the centerline when looking forward and starboard is the side of the boat to the right of the centerline when looking forward from the rear of the boat. Thus, the port side of the boat is always the left-hand half of the boat when facing forward, regardless of whether it is to the left or right of where you are standing. Facing to the rear does not make it the starboard side of the boat, even though it is now to your right.

I have purposely left LOA as an abbreviation, because that is how you will almost always encounter it in nautical drawings or literature. **LOA** stands for Length Over All and refers to the entire length of the boat. Some designers, when calculating LOA, include extensions to the hull, such as bow pulpits and swim platforms, while other designers will consider such features to be outside of the limits of the LOA. This is especially true of boats where such things are optional. Determine whether these features are included in the LOA before you start working. The addition of 3' of bow platform and 2' of swim platform to a 35' boat is a difference of almost 15% to the length of the boat, which could create a significant error factor when looking at LOA to Beam ratio (see below).

Beam is the width of the boat at its widest point. It is most commonly found at a point along the sheerline. When one speaks of a "beamy" boat they mean that the boat is wide relative to other boats. Two of the most important measurements for our purposes are LOA and Beam. They are usually available in any literature pertaining to a given boat.

Together, the LOA and Beam form a rectangle that defines the outer extents of the boats dimensions. When working with different scales, the **LOA:Beam ratio** (or percentage) of the width of the hull to its length stays constant no matter what scale you work in. To get the LOA:Beam ratio, divide the LOA by the beam. The length of the boat, in Image 3, is 2.78 times its width.

This ratio can be important when you don't have actual dimensions to work from. It is often the case that if your subject boat falls within a certain class of boats, you will find that others of the same class will have similar LOA:Beam ratios. If you can get dimensions from another boat of the same class, you may be able to reasonably guesstimate the beam of a boat if you know its LOA or vice versa.

Thus far, the terms that we have been discussing are fixed. A boat only has one LOA. It only has one beam. Other measurements change, sometimes quite significantly, depending upon which part of the hull they are taken from. Let's return to Figure 1 for a moment.

Freeboard is the vertical distance from any point along the sheerline to the waterline. It is the distance that you would have to fall from the edge of the boat to land in the water. Generally speaking, hulls of the type illustrated here have greater freeboard at the bow than at the stern. Freeboard information is sometimes listed in literature about a particular boat and can be helpful information when a good side view of the boat's sheerline is unavailable.

Deadrise is calculated, when looking at the hull from its ends, by measuring the angle between two lines: one running from the keel to the chine and the other parallel to the waterline (see the combined end views in Figure 1). On this type of hull the angle of deadrise taken at the deepest point of the keel is greater than it is at the stern. When a boat is referred to as having a "Deep-Vee" hull, it means that it has a great amount of deadrise at the lowest part of the keel. In other words: a large amount of deadrise means a great angle and deeper hull, while a small amount of deadrise means little angle and a shallow hull.

Knowing all of the terms we've covered in this chapter will make it easier to define the shapes of a boat.

Looking at a side view of a boat and using the waterline as a baseline, vertical distances can be calculated from it to any point on it the sheerline, chines or keel. From a top view, the sheerline and the chines can be measured, in a similar manner, by their relationships outward from centerline. From the end views, both the centerline and the waterline provide baseline references for the sheerline, chines, and keel. This is powerful information, but it's still somewhat unwieldy; we need some better methods of organization. We need to learn how certain kinds of drawings can be used to our advantage.

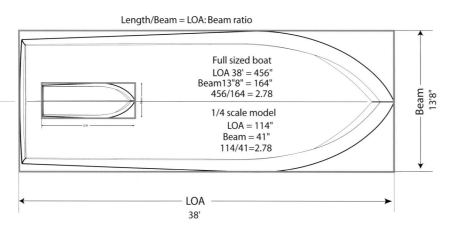

Length/Beam = LOA : Beam ratio

Full sized boat
LOA 38' = 456"
Beam 13"8" = 164"
456/164 = 2.78

1/4 scale model
LOA = 114"
Beam = 41"
114/41=2.78

Beam 13'8"

LOA 38'

Figure 3. The ratio of LOA:Beam does not change with scale. Note that for both sizes of boat it is 2.78.

Chapter 9
Understanding Mechanical Drawings

Part of being able to truly "see" a boat, or any other object that has significant shape characteristics means being able to understand the features of that shape and their spatial relationships to each other. Mechanical drawings are the most common means for conveying the language of dimensions. Being able to work with them, like all of the other skills that we discuss in this book, comes down to learning some basic principles and then getting practice using them. The basics of mechanical drawings are really very simple once you understand a few concepts. If you have difficulty with anything in this chapter, stop and mull things over. It will come...

The purpose of a mechanical drawing is to show a three-dimensional object within a two-dimensional picture. Making a mechanical drawing is called drafting. While most drafting is now done with the aid of computers, the fundamental principles behind it are the same as they have been for centuries. It is important to know that a computer is not required to understand or to make mechanical drawings.

Virtually everything manufactured for public consumption for the past century or so, has been designed via the use of some type of mechanical drawing. Such a drawing is where the initial concepts are first laid down. It is studied and reworked by various engineers and other specialists until the subject it describes meets acceptable criteria. Versions of the drawing are then used, in some form, on the work floor as plans for physically creating the objects depicted. The drawing is sometimes enhanced to create "artist's renderings" for use in sales and promotion. This means that everyone in the chain of manufacture has to understand and/or be able to create some type of mechanical drawing in order to do his or her job.

In addition to general manufacturing, mechanical drawings are used by people in a variety of other fields, including Building Architects, Electrical Engineers, Civil Engineers, Surveyors, and Scientists. The drawings generated in all of these fields have similarities and differences. Depending upon the subjects being depicted and the situations in which they are being used, drawings will be laid out differently, will prioritize different elements and will often have their own particular nomenclature. These differences are the result of practical necessity. We are particularly interested in the drawings of the people who design boats: Naval Architects. We will look at some of the important elements specific to naval architectural drawings in Chapter 16.

About Scale

Scale: One factor that makes drawing requirements vary pertains to the size of the subject. A drawing of an object that fits into a space that is 2" by 2" can be shown in "real-size," because it easily fits on a sheet of drafting paper. **Real-size**, in this context, means that the size of the drawing is the actual size of the object. Many things represented in mechanical drawings are much larger than available paper, such as cars, airplanes, houses, landscapes or boats.

In order to properly represent things that are larger than the size of the drawing paper, the image in the drawing must be scaled down. To **Scale** something means to represent it at a size that is different from real-size. An important rule is that, regardless of scale, *all proportions remain the same in the scaled version as in the original*. As a result, the scaled image retains all properties of a real-size image, except size. The concept of scale can be seen in the following image, which shows three boats, which –except for their size – are absolutely identical.

Whether drafting or model making, the principle of scale is the same. The formula for changing scale is that every original dimension is multiplied or divided by the exact same number. The result is a copy that is exactly the same proportionately, despite its different size. When we think of scaling things, we usually think of making them smaller. The opposite may be done with things that are very small, such as electronic parts, which may need to be scaled up, in order to reveal minute, or possibly invisible, details.

1/12th Scale

1/2 Scale

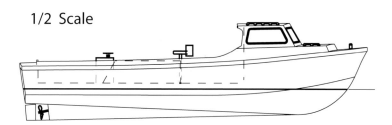

Full Size

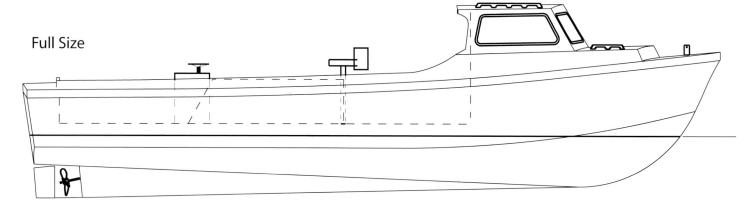

Figure 1. If we consider the largest of the three boats to be real-size, the mid-sized boat is shown at 1/2 scale. The smallest boat is shown at 1/12th scale or "one inch to the foot". Despite differences in size, all proportions remain exactly the same.

A frequently used scale for mechanical drawings is 1":1', or "one inch to the foot". This means that every inch of length in the drawing represents something that is 12" long at real size. Even though the drawing is not the size of the actual object, dimensional text is written as if the drawing were real-size. A tool made for easily converting measurements from scaled drawings is a triangular scale, which is a ruler that has been calibrated for the purpose. Each of its six edges is graduated for a different scale.

Among different types of model makers, there are different traditions established to determine the scales used. You may be familiar with some of the scales that are used by model train makers, including Z, N, HO, O, and G gauges. Marine models are usually made to some multiple or fraction of an inch relative to the foot. Common examples would be 1/2":1' , 1/4":1' or 1 1/2":1'.

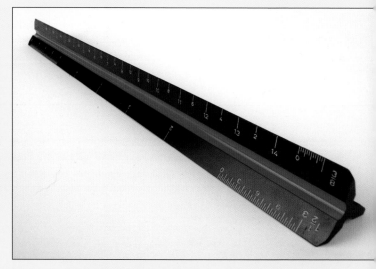

Figure 2. Each edge of the triangular scale is calibrated so that you can measure real size dimensions from scaled images.

3-View Drawing Layout

The location of views in a mechanical drawing: Mechanical drawings are different from freehand sketches in that they must include precise dimensional and structural information that can be measured directly from the drawing. If you like to draw, a sketch is an excellent tool for capturing the "essence" of your subject. Making a sketch is like taking notes of what you see. It can help you to understand how things relate to each other and force you to notice things that you otherwise might not, because of how it makes you focus on your subject. However, a sketch does not give you precise dimensional information. Also, a good sketch shows the subject as seen with perspective distortion. A mechanical drawing must be devoid of any such distortion.

Some mechanical drawings may contain incredibly large amounts of information that can quickly be overwhelming. When you first encounter such drawings, some things may be obvious while other things may make no sense and it may be hard to tell which things are relevant to your needs. A good drawing is simple and comprehensive. How to get what you need out of a drawing is easier when you understand a few basic points about layout. We will describe what's important in a good mechanical drawing piece by piece as we build one up.

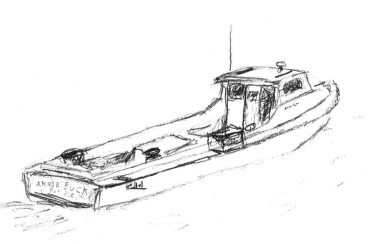

Figure 3. If you can, making a quick sketch is a good tool for deepening your sense of the things that make up a boat and their relative spatial locations in a way that is similar to taking notes in a classroom. The information in it is not sufficient for designing a highly accurate model, because it does not provide specific dimensions and it also contains distortion based on your viewing perspective.

We will use the nut shape in Figure 4 as our subject. It is a hexagonal block (6 sides) with a hole in it. The standard method for drawing basic objects is to show the object from three different viewpoints. It is known as a 3-view drawing. Three viewpoints can represent all of the information needed to understand the true shape of this simple object. The viewpoints are labeled top, front, and end.

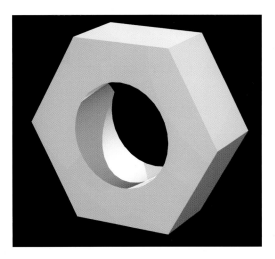

Figure 4.

This is not a drawing of three different objects; it is a drawing of one object from three different viewpoints. The viewpoint labeled front should be thought of as an anchor position, because the placements of the other two viewpoints are directly related to it. The front view is generally the view we see when looking at an object "broadside." The top view is how you see this object when looking from above. The end view is what we see when we turn the object sideways by 90 degrees.

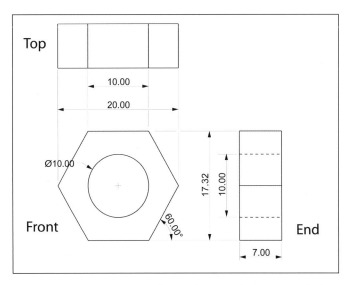

Figure 5. A clear and complete 3-view drawing of a hexagonal block with a hole through its center.

If we look at these views separately, we would see the following things from each one:

From the front:

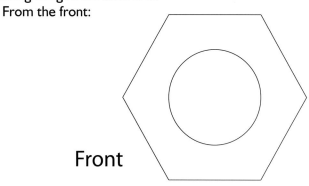

Front

Figure 6. Nut as viewed from the Front.

From the top:

Top

Figure 7. Nut as viewed from the top.

From the end:

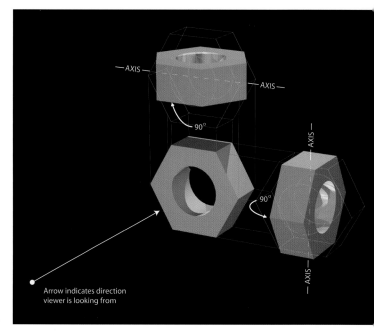

Figure 8. Nut as viewed from the end.

End

If you compare what you are seeing from each viewpoint, you will notice that there are similarities in each image, but no two are exactly the same.

For example, the widths are the same between the top and front views; not in the end view. The heights of the front and end views are the same, but not in the top view. The diameter of the hole remains the same in all views; however, its representation varies from a circle in the front view, to dotted lines in the end view. The top view, alone, provides no evidence that there is a hole.

This illustrates two important points:

1. It is not possible to display all of the object's information in a single view, and

2. A significant amount of information is the same from view to view.

Clarity and comprehensiveness are very important. A properly laid out 3-view drawing accomplishes both. It does so by aligning each view in such a way that when a dimension is determined in one view, it is known to be true for the others. This reduces the amount of clutter in the drawing by reducing redundant information.

Figure 9. Another way of envisioning the positions of views in a 3-view drawing. See text.

The following image can be used to better understand how the views are set up:

The typical 3-view drawing is usually set up as shown in Figure 9. Yes, we have already stated that a 3-view drawing represents a single object from three viewpoints, but for illustrative purposes, it may make things clearer to picture three identical objects, each set at different positions and angles. The arrow and ball at the left of the picture shows the perspective from which the observer is looking. The lower left nut represents the front view, which again should be thought of as the anchor position. To the right of the object representing the front position we have placed an identical nut, but we have rotated it 90 degrees around the axis shown. The blue outline represents the object's original position. The angle of the new nut is perpendicular to the blue outline and the end is what now faces the observer, providing an end view. Note that while the new view reveals a significantly different view, there have been no changes to any vertical dimensions. This can be verified by looking at the horizontal red connecting lines between the two nuts.

Similarly, we have placed another nut above the anchor nut. Again the blue lines represent the original position and again we rotate the nut 90 degrees around its respective axis. This time, the result is that the top of the object faces the observer. Although the view is quite different from the front view, all horizontal dimensions remain the same as in the front view. You can check this by looking at the red vertical connecting lines.

Note the resulting "L" shaped positioning of the views. One way of clarifying the drawing is to reduce the number of times redundant information needs to be shown. By placing the views so that such information is in alignment, horizontal dimensions written for the front and top views are known to be the same and do not need to be written separately for each view.

The same is true for vertical dimensions between the front and end views.

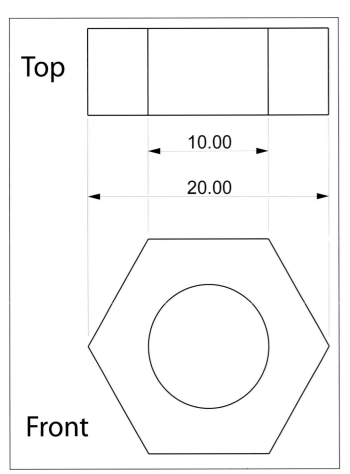

Figure 10. Isolating the front and top views show that horizontal dimensions are the same for each and how they line up as indicated by the vertical lines. This means that dimensions only have to be written once to represent both views.

Reassembling these views together we now have the following drawing:

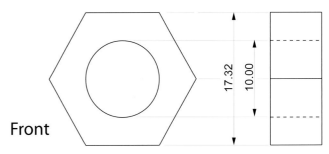

Figure 11. If we isolate the front and end views in the same way, the same is true, except that it is the vertical dimensions that remain the same. Again, this is demonstrated by the horizontal connecting lines.

The drawing in Figure 12 provides a complete and concise description of our nut. If you follow the lighter vertical and horizontal lines, you can see which dimensions are carried over from view to view. These are places where a single dimensional description serves two views. A good example is the height of 17.32, which pertains to the front and end views. Others are the widths of 20 and 10 that pertain to the front and top views.

A ruler, especially a clear one, is a good tool to have when reading such drawings. It can be used to follow lines in one view and see how they relate to another. For instance, if you align a ruler with the innermost vertical lines of the top view, you will see that they meet the edges of the hole in the front view, revealing that the diameter of the hole is also 10; the same as the width between those two lines.

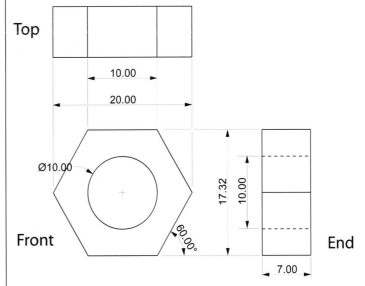

Figure 12. This is a basic, but complete, 3-view drawing of our nut.

Lines, edges, and other features that are inside or on the opposite side of the object so that they are obscured in the view shown are represented by dotted lines. The dotted lines in the end view represent the position of the hole within the nut. There is no visible representation of the hole in the top view. This is because the visible edges in the top view, being the same width as the diameter of the hole, obscure the dotted lines that would represent the position of the hole. Thus, the dotted lines in the end view are the only way of knowing that the hole runs all of the way through the nut.

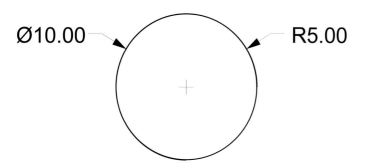

Figure 13. The dimensions of holes are indicated by either diameter, to the left, or radius, to the right. The cross hatch marks the exact center.

Note the circle with a slash through it followed by the number 10. It refers to diameter and the cross mark in the center of the hole is an important part of the notation. Where they cross shows where the point of a drill bit would be placed to cut the hole. If the diameter symbol was replaced by an R, the mark would have the same meaning, except that instead of diameter, the reference would be to radius. The meaning of radius, being the distance from the center of the circle to its edge, which is always half of a circle's diameter, means that the measurement would be 5. At the lower right of the front view is the usual method of marking angles. For every angle there is at least one counter angle. If the angle measurement were made inside of the nut, the result would be 120 degrees instead of 60.

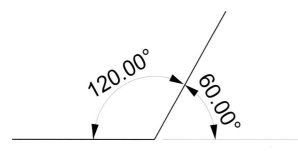

Figure 14. A counter angle to the angle of 60 degrees between the sides of this nut would be 120 degrees if the measurements were taken from inside the nut instead of the outside.

Why 3 Views?

What is important is not the number of views; it is the need for a sufficient number of views to capture all necessary information. A 4-view image, which, as the name implies, adds a fourth view, can include any other viewpoint. It may be a close-up of some detail, but probably most often includes a perspective angle, which can sometimes elucidate the object's form in a way that is easier to understand as compared to the sometimes too sterile mechanical images.

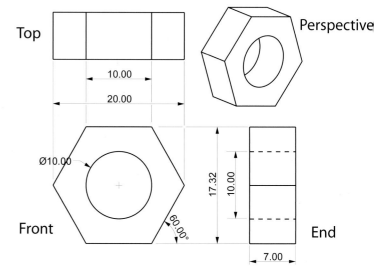

Figure 15. A 4-view drawing with an added perspective view. Other possible views could be made of any other information that needs specific clarification.

Note that the perspective view does not line up with the other views. Its scale has nothing to do with the other views. It does, however, present a more natural looking image of the object, which can help to answer certain questions that might arise. It is similar to adding a sketch to the drawing.

Missing Information Can Lead to False Conclusions

My father, in attempting to teach me about what can happen when insufficient information is shown, teased me with a problem similar to the following: Given the information shown in the top and end views, what does the object look like?

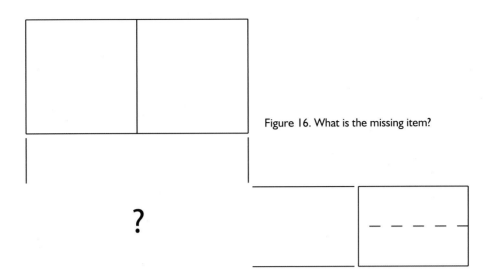

Figure 16. What is the missing item?

?

Thinking that I was pretty smart, I came up with what I knew was the simple answer. I was correct, partially. He then began to draw for me possibility after possibility, including the following:

There are also many more possibilities... You will see that all of these and many more shapes could fill the position in question. This shows why we need sufficient views to really understand what we are seeing. For most objects, three views are adequate.

Play with this a bit. Make some copies of Figure 16 to play with. Using the shapes shown in Figure 17 as examples, try to fill in the lines that define the missing front view. It's not difficult if you remember to extend horizontal lines from the end view and vertical lines from the top view. See if you can imagine any other shapes that might fit into the missing view.

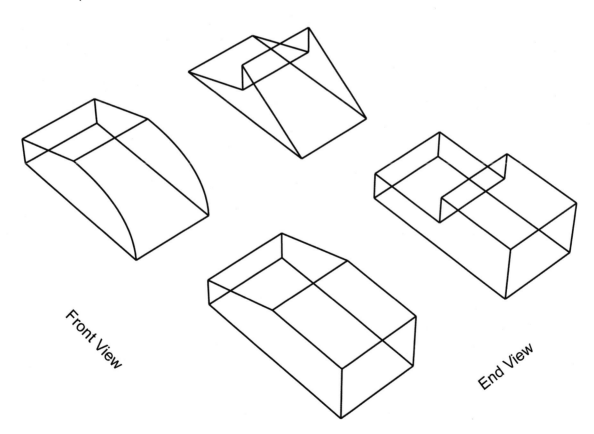

Figure 17. These are only a few of the possibilities that could fit into the questioned space. You may want to try to see if you can come up with others yourself.

Chapter 10
Measuring Tools and Techniques

Measuring is among the most important types of skills to master for a model maker. Measuring is done during research when taking measurements from drawings. Measuring is done when setting up your plans. Measuring done during construction is especially important, whether you are trying to make the first straight edge on a piece of rough lumber or to check the thickness of a thread for rigging.

Measuring involves more than just determining the distance between points. It means being able to draw straight lines, to compare curvatures, to measure diameter, to determine "square" vs. angles, or to determine parallelism and to perform other related techniques. None of these techniques is really difficult. They do require that you learn a few standard methods, so that you end up with the same results as someone else and that you get the same results each time you make the same measurement. In some cases the trick for making the measurement might be in having a special tool for the purpose.

Measurements done in the real-size world can be done with the usual array of tools, including tape measures, carpenter's squares, levels, and other familiar equipment. However, when we start to work at reduced sizes, something interesting happens. We are not only scaling down our subject, but we need to scale down our tolerance for error as well. If we are off by 1" on the LOA of a boat that is 20' long, it is not very noticeable. If we are off by 1" on a 20" model, this represents a pretty serious amount. At real size the error is $1/240^{th}$ of the length of the boat. At 1":1' scale, this error increases to $1/20^{th}$ or 5% of the LOA (Length Over All). This means understanding that some of the measuring tools that we use for real-size work must be used more carefully and in some cases may not be accurate enough for working in miniature. Not having an awareness of the right tools is often the reason that some things seem impossible.

Figure 1. Accuracy is important. An error of only 5% in length, but not other dimensions, can have a significant effect, distorting the overall shape of the boat. The red outline is not true to scale.

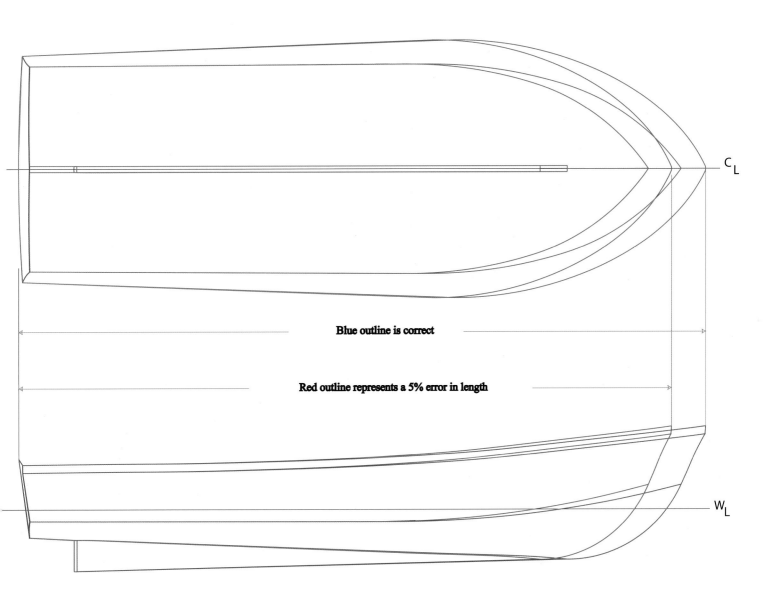

Blue outline is correct

Red outline represents a 5% error in length

C_L

W_L

Most of the work of measuring involves making marks of some kind. Standard wood pencils should be sharp for paper, slightly rounder for wood, but able to make consistently thin lines. We find that a long tipped mechanical pencil with .9mm lead works very well for most purposes. The long tip provides consistency when following straight edges. The .9mm diameter makes readable, but thin lines and does not tend to dig into soft woods. Do not use ink with wood; it can seep through grain and become irremovable.

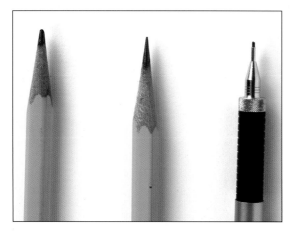

Figure 2. Left: pencil slightly rounded for woodworking. Center: a sharp tip for making detailed drawings. Right: a good mechanical pencil does not need as much tip maintenance.

Have you ever noticed that the line of your pencil never really touches the line of your straightedge? Compensate by moving your straightedge slightly so that your line is in the correct place. An old draftsman's trick is to also rotate your pencil as you make your line, so that your pencil tip wears evenly, instead of making one part more prominent than another.

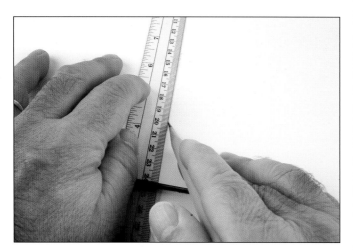

Figure 3. There is a space between the tip of the pencil and the edge of the ruler. This offsets the line from where it should be if the ruler's edge is where the line should be. Base ruler placement on where the line should be, not the ruler itself.

For general measuring of real-sized items, such as boats, tape measures are important, including very long ones. For design and shop work, where tolerances need to be much tighter, they are most useful for general measuring of raw stock; they are not good where close tolerances are important.

Rulers: Wooden rulers are just not accurate enough for model work. Both metal and plastic rulers are printed, etched or molded precisely from materials that retain accuracy. Clear rulers are excellent for most applications, but can be ruined if used as straightedges with cutting tools. Use metal, or metal edged rulers when working with blades. Another good ruler to have is a three-sided scale ruler. Its divisions conform to various common scales used in model making and drafting and you can measure inches and feet directly from scaled plans without having to make calculations.

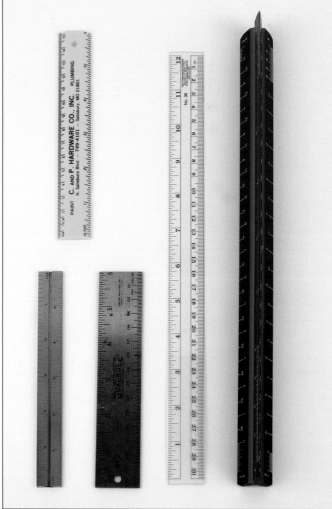

Figure 4. This is a good collection of rulers for model making; clockwise from top left: a general purpose accurate plastic ruler, a clear plastic ruler which allows visibility beneath it, an architect's scale which is graduated in standard scales, a metal ruler with non-skid cork backing and a sturdy 6" metal rule.

When working with any ruler, your marks should always be made deliberately at the centers of division lines. Sometimes the scale of a ruler does not begin exactly at zero and you must take this into account. On some rulers it is obvious; on others, the end of the ruler may be incorrect by as much as +/- 1/16th". This can be checked by placing another ruler alongside the one in question; align any other inch-to-inch marks of the reference ruler with the 1-inch mark and see where the end of the ruler falls. The difference determines whether compensation, and how much, is needed. When measuring from the end, do not trace the end; an error will be created by the offset of your pencil tip.

Squares: Achieving proper angles is a very important part of both drafting and model making. Dominating our world of angles is the "right angle," which is the same as "perpendicular," which is the same as "square," all of which refer to an angle of 90 degrees between two lines or surfaces. There are a myriad of tools for making things square. These tools include: carpenter's squares, T-squares, machinist's squares, and combination squares, just to name a few.

Squares make drafting possible. The squares used for drafting require the use of a drafting board or table. It does not have to be fancy. It is usually made from high quality plywood. It must be rigid, but with a surface just soft enough to allow a compass point to properly set in. It must also be perfectly square with all edges sanded smooth. The T-square must be able to slide perfectly along the left edge.

Figure 5. Checking to see if the end of a ruler is "true." The lower ruler's end is at zero; although the end of the top ruler is not at the zero mark, it is clearly marked, so mistakes are unlikely.

Figure 6. These are just a few of the many types of squares that we use on a regular basis. The large black square is a T-square. Left to right above it are small 45/45/90, large 30/60/90, and small 30/60/90 degree draftsman's angle templates. Below the T-square from left to right: large and small combination squares, large and small machinist's squares, a rosewood tri-square, and a carpenter's square.

The basis of drafting is simple. It is to make accurate and descriptive lines. All horizontals must be perfectly horizontal. All verticals must be perfectly vertical. All other straight lines must be straight and drawn at proper angles. The T-square makes it easy to make perfect horizontals; the angle templates in conjunction with the T-square make it easy to make perfect verticals, as well as 30, 45, and 60-degree angles. Other lines and curves are made using straightedges, protractors, French curves, compasses, and other templates.

Figure 8. All vertical lines are made using an angle template in conjunction with the T-square. This means that the T-square must have good contact with the edge of the drafting board and the template must be in good contact with the T-square. If a line was made on the other side of the template shown, it would be 60 degrees from horizontal. If the square were to be rotated to the right 90 degrees, it would be set up for a 30-degree line. Likewise, the 45-degree template provides 45- and 90-degree angles. Lines at these angles can be made anywhere in the drawing space by sliding the T-square and template to the desired location.

Figure 7. The basis of drafting is to make lines as you want them to be made, the foremost line being horizontal. The T-square is the tool that makes perfect horizontal lines possible. It is used by sliding its head along the left side of a drafting board or table so that horizontal lines can be made anywhere within the drawing space. Note that the paper has also been aligned with the same T-square and secured with masking tape so that it does not move while the drawing is being made.

Squares in the Shop: We prefer machinist's squares and small combination squares in the workshop. The larger types of squares may come in handy during measuring sessions of full-sized boats, but tend to be oversized for model work. Squares, like other tools, can be damaged and lose accuracy over time. Protect them from bending or impact. Machinist's squares tend to be the sturdiest and are made to very high tolerances.

Figure 9. Of all the squares above, these three get the most use in our shop. From left to right: 6" machinist's square, 6" combination square, and 3" machinist's square.

One of the secrets of good drafting is to make your initial lines very lightly. You want to be able to cleanly erase anything that will get in the way of clearly understanding your drawing later and, not that it ever happens to us mind you, but there might occasionally be a mistake that needs correcting. After you are satisfied with your lines, you can darken those that you feel are important.

They are also the tool of choice when making adjustments to the blades or fences of power tools. Combination squares not only provide a 90-degree angle, but also a 45-degree angle along with a ruler and straightedge. Some combination squares have other accessories built in such as marking awls and levels. For quick checking of square angles in situations when you don't happen to have the proper tool handy, many everyday items, such as credit cards or sheets of paper also have very accurate 90-degree angles between their edges.

For measuring non-square angles, a bevel gauge and protractor are usually the best tools. To copy an existing angle, loosen the blade on the bevel gauge and place the part of the object with the angle to be measured between the blade and the block of the gauge. Tighten the blade. Recheck your piece, in case the blade moved on tightening. To determine the angle, align the block of the bevel gauge with the protractor's bottom edge and slide it until the edge of the blade runs through the center mark of the protractor. Where the edge lines up with the dial of the protractor is the angle in degrees. Note that there are usually two numbers at every 10th degree. If your angle is less than 90 degrees, use the smaller number. If your angle is greater than 90 degrees use the larger number. Note that this difference also affects the direction in which you count any additional degrees on the dial. You can also work in reverse, setting the bevel gauge to a known angle using the protractor and then transferring the angle to your work.

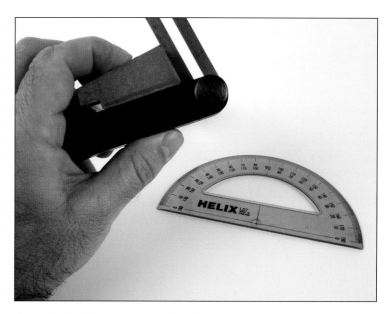

Figure 11. Bevel gauge set to angle to be measured.

Figure 12. To calculate the angle captured by the bevel gauge, the blade must be positioned so that its edge runs through the crosshairs of the protractor. The correct reading is 77 degrees, because it is less than 90 degrees (see text).

Figure 10. Bevel gauge, protractor, and piece with angle to be measured. Blade of gauge is loosened and tightened by turning the knob.

If you find yourself using the same non-square angles frequently, it helps to carefully cut angle blocks. These blocks can be used to quickly change tool settings or to make a fast measurement. Be sure to mark them in a way that you can tell quickly what the angle is without confusion.

One rule to bear in mind about angles: when you change scale by changing the sizes of objects, angles do not change. Any angle present in a real size subject is always the correct angle for your model.

Compass and Dividers: Dividers, a type of calipers, are very powerful tools. While they do not read out measurements as other tools do, the distance between their points can easily be compared to a ruler or other measuring standard. They can be set for a measurement within construction plans and this measurement can be directly transferred to an item under construction. In conjunction with a straightedge, a measurement can be repeated an infinite number of times with perfect accuracy.

Figure 13. Despite the wear, this angle block is still good, even though it is over 10 years old. It makes quick work of setting up miter saw and band saw angles.

Dividers differ in type of tips they have; in addition to straight dividers others have special tips for making inside and outside measurements. Some dividers are designed to hold their measurements better, which is determined by the type of hinge and fulcrum they have as well as whether or not they have a screw adjuster. Those without are usually meant for lighter duty on the drafting board and can easily lose their measurement if touched on their legs, while those meant for shop work are sturdier and usually have screw adjustments or locking mechanisms.

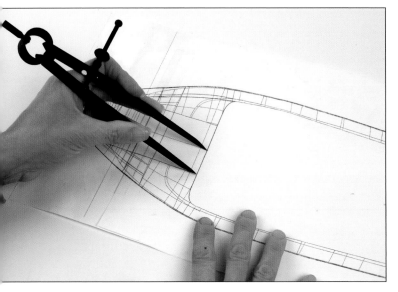

Figure 14. Straight dividers being set to a drawing to transfer a dimension to a model

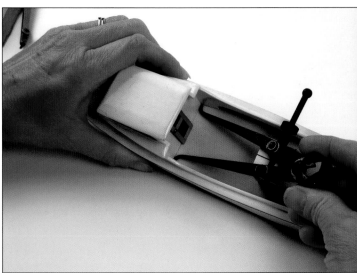

Figure 15. Inside calipers set to an interior dimension for comparison to a measuring tool.

Figure 16. Outside calipers being used to capture the diameter of a rod.

A compass is generally thought of as a tool used to make circles. This is true, but in many cases it can be used like dividers, with the added capability of making pencil marks. Compasses come with the same types of hinges and adjusters as dividers, but have the ability to accommodate different pencil, ink or divider tips. Quality compasses can be used as dividers, but because of their interchangeable construction are sometimes bulkier and not always practical for tight spaces. A trammel is a variation of compass that can be used to measure larger radii. It consists of a long bar with a point at one end and marking device at the other.

Compasses are used to draw circles. They are really dividers with a graphite tip for marking. A circle is one of the most powerful shapes that one can imagine. Any point on a circle is the same distance from the center of it as any other point on that circle. There is no way to cover all of the possibilities that this can lead to, but here are a few. Figure 18 shows some ways that the compass can be used to gain information that goes far beyond simple circles, when used in conjunction with straight horizontal lines and straight vertical lines.

In figure 18a, horizontal and vertical lines that touch a circle at the numbered points make a square, because all of the lines are of equal length. To determine a 45 degree angle without other tools, run a straight line from the center of the circle to one of the corners, or diagonally from corner to corner. In figure 18b, we see that any straight line drawn at any angle that begins at the center of a circle and ends on its ring is the same length. This is especially helpful when multiple lines of the same length go in different directions. Rather than measure each one with a ruler, use a compass. Figure 18c shows how to draw a scale with equivalent spacing. Starting with a straight line (it could be at any angle), draw a circle as shown at position on line c1. Place the center of the subsequent circles at the intersections that are created each time a circle is made, in this case to number 6. C2 shows the result if the tops and bottoms of the circles are erased. There are always two more lines than there are centers. The distance between the scale markings is equal to the radius you set for your compass. Figure 18d, starts in a similar way. D1 shows three circles, set up as in the previous example. In d2 we add two lines; the first runs from the center of the leftmost circle, labeled start point 1 and run it through the upper intersection of the left and middle circles, labeled pass-through point 1. If we do the same in reverse, drawing a line from start point 2 through pass-through point 2, we see a triangle take form. The sides and angles of the triangle that is formed are all equal to each other. All interior angles are 60 degrees. This is a good start if you are designing something with 3 spokes, such as a propeller or a steering wheel.

Thus, using a compass, we have found a square, a means of simplifying certain measurements, how to divide a scale equally and how to make a triangle where all sides and angles are equal.

Many people I've known like to impress others by throwing around the term "thousandths of an inch". It certainly used to impress me. It seems like an unfathomable number, like "billion". Actually, at this point in the world of technology, thousandths of inches are behemoth to some people. Most models are really not that accurate, but being able to measure at a level of accuracy of one thousandth of an inch (.001") can make your work much finer than if you are limited to an accuracy of 1/32" (.03125"), which is the smallest division of most rulers. No matter how good your measuring skills are, there is always a likelihood of some error and the closer tolerances you try to achieve the lower your overall amount of error is likely to be.

Figure 17. The simple, but elegant art of drawing a circle with a compass

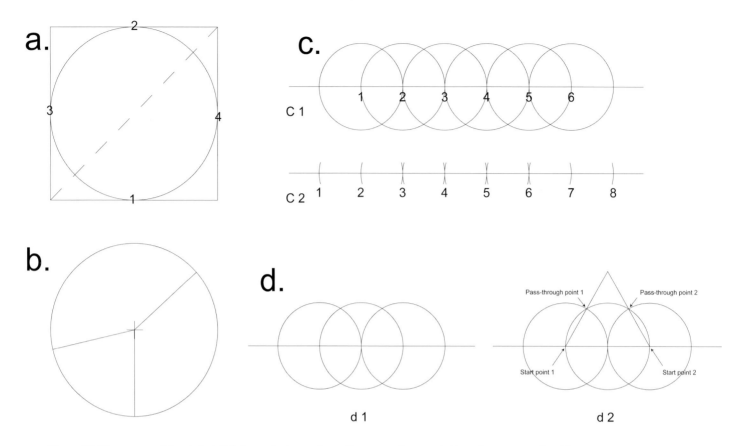

Figure 18. The power of the circle is lightly touched upon here. Here are a few good things that you can do with a compass: *see text*.

There are relatively inexpensive tools for measuring at these tolerances. The one that we use the most is dial calipers. Dial calipers generally have three options for measurement. The jaws are used for taking outside dimensions; the points opposite the jaws can be used to take inside dimensions, such as the diameter of a hole. At the bottom of the tool is a rail that extends to measure depth.

Like dividers, they can be used to transfer dimensions from drawings, but they measure, which dividers cannot do. Once the measurement is taken, there is a setscrew for locking the calipers at that reading. The dial displays your measurement in thousandths of an inch as a decimal number. A measurement taken with any of the three means can be transferred using any of the others. Thus, if the jaws are used to measure the diameter of a cylinder, the opposite points can be used to measure the inside diameter of a hole to see if that cylinder would fit into it. To read the measurement, first read the larger numbers along the body and then add what is on the dial to that number. Older calipers of this type are read using a Vernier scale. Unless you are familiar with the Vernier system, you should stick to the dial version. Recently, digital versions have become available, but are a bit more costly.

Figure 19. Dial Calipers, showing jaws at upper left, points to the right of them, and depth rail at the bottom.

Micrometers are used for high tolerance measurements of round stock and for measuring thickness of flat materials. They also come in versions with numerical or Vernier readouts. We recommend numerical readouts for these tools, as well. Micrometers and dial calipers are often found at auto supply stores.

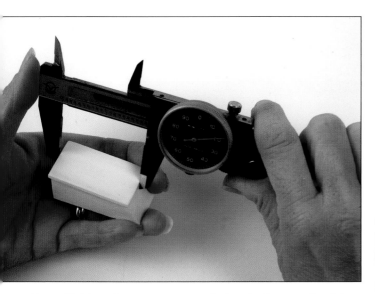

Figure 20. Using the jaws to measure the length of a motor box lid. The reading is 1.919".

Figure 21. Using the points to measure the narrowest width of pilothouse gingerbread. It reads 1.662".

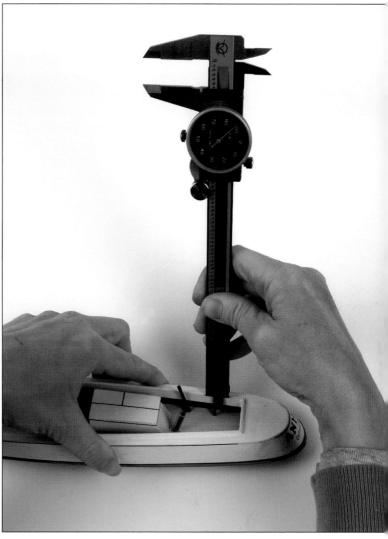

Figure 22. Measuring the depth from the top of the coaming to the floor. The distance is .587".

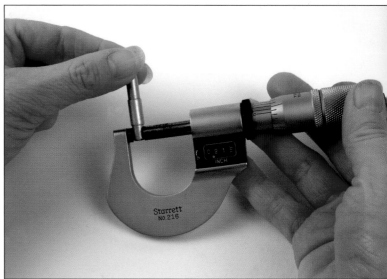

Figure 23. Using a micrometer to measure aluminum tubing. The reading equals 7/32".

An excellent and simpler tool for determining the diameters of tubing, rods, screws, and drill bits is a drill gauge. Better ones not only show the bit size in decimal numbers and fractions, but also show the gauge size number, which is how most very small drill bits are designated.

Looking at the numerals on the drill gauge reminds me that magnification tools are essential. We use a magnifying lamp, hand-held magnifying glasses, as well as "cheaters"—otherwise known as magnified reading glasses.

Figure 24. Drill gauge being used to measure the diameter of a brass rod.

There are times when you must draw curved lines. In order to do so without kinks and especially when you are trying to make curves that are natural, there are tools and methods for doing so. An example of a natural curve would be that made by a wooden plank that forms the side of a boat's hull. A universally accepted set of templates called "French Curves" have been used for ages for this purpose. They are used to find and trace the curve that is able to pass through a series of points, like a "connect the dots" game. This connecting of the dots is also known as "fairing". Another way of fairing with drawings on paper is to place pins or small nails at measurement points and use a thin piece of wood or plastic, taking advantage of its behavior relative to those points. When it is in place, it can be traced and the proper line is obtained. Sometimes in design it is discovered that a certain set of points cannot be faired

and the locations of the points must be recalculated. This recalculation can involve significant work. Better to find out at the drawing board than later.

Figure 25. Some examples of the wide variety of French Curves that are available.

Tracing paper is good for transferring not only dimensions, but can be used to trace contours and other lines, which can then be copied at a different scale with a copy machine or scanner and printer. Similarly, carbon paper or one of its variants can be used to trace plans onto wood or other material for cutting. It is important to affix it and the plans well to the material being copied to, so that there is no movement, which would result in distortion or an outright change in shape.

Finally, for any time that you will need to repeatedly measure a set of dimensions, especially if the shapes are odd, consider making your own templates.

There are many other tools and techniques that can be used for measuring and we cannot fit all of them here, but keep your eyes open for them. Some are better than others and your experiences will determine what you prefer. Note what other artisans use. There is much information to be gained by watching machinists, train and airplane modelers, cabinetmakers, jewelers, and others for whom measurement is an important part of what they do.

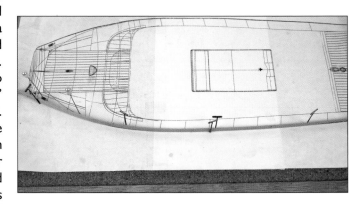

Figure 26. One method of fairing a curve.

Chapter 11
About the ANNIE BUCK

David and Ann have good reason to be proud. They belong to that group of extremely tough and hard working people known in this part of the world as "Watermen". All you have to do is shake David's hand to know that he has more than earned that right. His hands are leathery, strong and steady, and bespeak a lifetime of good, honest work.

There aren't too many new watermen. It's a hard life and requires a great deal of knowledge about the area, with its sometimes dangerous, shallow waters; a hand on the pulse of the health of the "Bay" and its inhabitants; an understanding of market prices and negotiations; the knowledge and ability to captain and maintain a boat, often old and in need of nurturing; the inner strength to weather the tough times and to be prudent in the good ones and the outer toughness to work in temperature ranges from well below freezing to over 100 degrees. There aren't too many new watermen because there are easier ways to make a living. This is one simple explanation.

The fact of the matter is that there aren't a whole lot of new watermen because it takes a lot of knowledge and hardiness to be one. Success takes a lot more than wanting to try it out. Most of the watermen today descended from previous generations of watermen who learned and then passed on their secrets to their children. These days, things aren't as plentiful as they used to be. As with other people involved in the harvesting of seafood—lobstermen, fin fisherman, scallopers, shrimpers—and as it is for many who work in agriculture, they are, more and more, pointing their children, not in the direction of continuing such a hard way of life, but to get a college education and to do something else. It's not hard to understand this when you hear David get up at 3:00 a.m. every morning, or during the times of the year that you don't see him during the week, because he and his boat have to live where the oysters are.

It is not proper to refer to a waterman as a fisherman. There are some watermen who harvest fish, but most watermen do relatively little of that. The primary seafood species, but certainly not the only ones, caught in the Chesapeake Bay are blue crabs, which are caught during the warm months, and oysters, which are harvested in the colder months.

The Chesapeake Bay is a large body of water, centered on the U.S. East Coast. Its mouth opens into the Atlantic Ocean. In addition to the tides ebbing and flowing salt water from the Atlantic Ocean at its southern opening, several major rivers also feed the Bay, including the Susquehanna and its vast watershed stretches high into upstate New York, hundreds of miles North. As a result of the many major rivers flowing into it, the Chesapeake Bay receives a great inflow of fresh water from mid-winter to late spring from the melting of snows. The ratio of fresh water inflow from rivers to salt water from the ocean causes change in the salinity of the Bay from season to season, which is critical to its ecosystem. The water of the Chesapeake is "brackish" or somewhat salty, but not salt water as is found in the ocean. In fact, the balance of its ecosystem, with its regular changes in salinity throughout the year makes it the perfect nursery for many species that are more famously harvested in other waters, notably Striped Bass (called "rockfish" in these parts) and Bluefish, that migrate to New England as they get older and larger.

The length of the total shoreline of the Bay and its tributaries is greater than the roughly 3,500 miles distance it takes to cross the entire US. This is because of the many rivers, peninsulas, and islands that make it up. In relatively recent geological history, the Bay's features have been changing with islands disappearing and peninsulas becoming islands, due to tidal conditions and storm activity. The entire region, as with most other marine regions, undergoes constant change.

Figure 1.

Much of the water in the Chesapeake is relatively shallow. There is a vantage point near our home where you can look across the Bay at what seems like a small ocean. It is interesting to note that the depth of water out as far as two miles is no more than chest deep. The average diurnal (twice daily) tidal change in this region is 18," which contrasts with other seafood areas such as New England, where the average diurnal tidal change in many locations is 9' or more.

For the Waterman, shallow water is good for access to reach crabs and oysters. Conversely, a potential consequence of using a boat in shallow water is the possibility of running aground. This dictates that a boat working in such waters must have a relatively small amount of draft and virtually rules out the possibility of using a deep displacement hulled boat. Knowing this tells you something about a boat that works under these conditions without even seeing it.

The combination of shallow depth and the presence of many land features, including peninsulas and islands, which compound wave activity and concentrate the flow of current in the channels between them, sometimes results in a very hard chop and dangerous conditions, with

characteristics that are different from those found in other bodies of water. During the summer, the bay is notorious for "pop-up" thunderstorms, which are sudden, intense storms that may not last more than twenty minutes, but can cause nightmarish conditions on the water. These storms are often classified by The National Weather Service as "Severe". This leads to another feature of workboats in the Chesapeake: they need to be able to go fast in order to get home quickly. Planing hulls are better able to do this.

The best boat for the Chesapeake is not necessarily the best boat elsewhere. In fact, it might perform poorly in the conditions found in other parts of the world. There is no boat that is perfect for all conditions in all places and indeed, some that are perfect in their particular domain are particularly unsuitable in others.

Those of us who work indoors don't spend a lot of time thinking about the sturdiness or safety of the place where we work. That safety is a given. Anyone who operates a boat professionally needs to have that same kind of confidence. Some days the water is as still as a mirror; on others, various storm and wind conditions can make you feel like you are in the mouth of a lion, with high breaking waves, biting icy gusts and/or other conditions that can reduce visibility and control and if the boat is not up to the task, the results can be deadly. While all commercially made boats must meet stringent Coast Guard standards for loading, resistance to capsizing, and several other factors, most pleasure boats are not expected to be operated five or six days a week, nor are they expected to be used in the winter, or during weather that may frequently not be "pleasurable".

One property of all good workboats: they are built to be sturdy. If you can do so with the owner's permission, gently thump the flare of a pleasure boat with the bottom of your fist and you are likely to hear a nice low pitched drum sound. Do the same with a workboat and it is usually far more solid with virtually no resonance. This is not meant, in any way, to belittle the qualities of pleasure boats; it is simply that workboats see a lot more stress than pleasure boats and the requirement of greater sturdiness is another characteristic that helps us to understand the boat better.

themselves. If someone has the ability, as they've certainly proven, it is a cost effective way of getting more boat for the money. In addition, they were able to build her to suit their needs perfectly. It took months and months of carpentry, laying of fiberglass, the installation of cables, electrical wiring, steering gear, fuel tank, and many other things until one of the last steps—the transfer of the nearly new diesel from their old boat brought *ANNIE BUCK* to life.

Figure 3. The *ANNIE BUCK* returns home after a winter of oyster dredging more than 50 miles from home. You can see her mast and boom, used to raise and lower the oyster dredge. The plank on the side protects the hull from damage from contact with the dredge.

If you have never seen a boat under construction before, you may find it to be an eye-opening experience. There are so many methods of construction that we never tire of watching, because every one is different. Many maritime museums have ongoing boat building programs where you can watch the process and in some cases participate. Despite the fact that building a model is not usually building an exact miniature of the real boat, the methods are often similar. For instance, plank on bulkhead construction in a model is similar to plank on frame construction of a real boat. Sometimes getting a look at how that plank on frame boat was made answers otherwise tricky questions about how to approach your own model. In any case, it is fascinating if you like boats.

Figure 2. At this beach, near Tilghman Island, the Bay is approximately 8 miles wide. From this vantage point out about 2 miles, the water is no more than chest deep. In this winter photo you can see extensive ice floe. Watermen work throughout the year. Sometimes they must deal with severe conditions of heat and cold. The boat they use must be sturdy and reliable under all conditions that they could face.

The *ANNIE BUCK* is David and Ann's boat. It is by no means their first, but it is certainly something special. It is a Chesapeake Bay "Deadrise," the most widely used class of workboat in the Chesapeake. We know a bit about her because we watched as she arrived at David and Ann's house as just the fiberglass shell that makes up her hull. Because new boats are very expensive, they opted to start with a pre-built hull and construct the remainder of the boat

Figure 4. The *ANNIE BUCK* started as a molded fiberglass hull, much like this one. It is interesting to see just the hull as a sub-assembly of the boat, awaiting the addition of other sub-assemblies, such as the deck, superstructure, power, and other gear.

The origin of the word "deadrise" is one that we have been unable to fully pin down, even after speaking with many boat builders that have built them, museum experts, historians, and watermen. As you will recall, the term "deadrise," as used in naval architecture, refers to the angle of a line drawn from chine to keel and greater deadrise implies greater draft (see chapter 8 on measurement features). When you look at modern deadrises, which are designed specifically to be shallow draft boats, they tend to have relatively low angles of deadrise. Based on the information that we have gathered over the years, we believe that the name may come, at least partially, from a feature that belongs to older examples of deadrises. Wooden deadrises have **transverse planked** bottoms, which is to say that the planks run from the keel outwards towards the chines. Other wooden boats commonly have longitudinal planking, which runs fore to aft. You will see in older deadrises (and some new wooden ones) that at the bow they appear to have an extreme degree of deadrise, but are crafted in a way that does not give the boat a deep draft overall. You will also see this type of planking and bow on some other famous Chesapeake boat types, including skipjacks and draketails, the latter being a type of deadrise with a rounded and downward sloping stern instead of a wide transom.

Figure 6. The name "deadrise" is a tricky one to understand, when thinking of boats whose modern designs tend to have relatively low amounts of deadrise angle. When you look at a more traditional wooden deadrise and the lines formed by the edges of its transverse planks, however, you will see that the first half dozen, or so, planks have extreme angles of deadrise, making for a very sharp bow.

Figure 5. *ANNIE BUCK* hauled out for maintenance. David and Ann built everything on her but the shell of the hull. The result is an extremely fine Chesapeake Bay Deadrise.

At this point, it should be evident that some good research information about a boat can be ascertained by getting to know what that boat is required to do and about things that are generally common to its class. We will put some of these factors together here in order to get a better image of the *Annie Buck* and why she is built the way that she is, based upon the work she is used for.

Deadrises have features that, when combined together, are virtually definitive of the type. They must be able to work in shallow water, which dictates that they must have a shallow draft. Displacement hulls are, by definition, deep draft hulls and are not practical. Deadrises have planing hulls that are relatively flat at the stern and have sharp chines along the sides of the hull. They are almost always powered by inboard motors, which are large and must be located more or less centrally in the boat. A boat with shallow draft does not have a lot of space beneath the waterline. This means that the motor must protrude above the floor and is housed in a motor box. The motor box is usually rectangular shaped, the top often serving as a worktable.

Crabbing and oystering both require open work and storage space and the majority of the boat is dedicated to the cockpit. Deadrises are worked by one and occasionally two persons, requiring operation of the boat from the work area and you will find a control station in the rear of the boat in addition to the helm in the pilot house. The *ANNIE BUCK* has a control pod with a steering wheel and throttle. Many deadrises are steered by means of a steering stick, rather than a steering wheel. The work of crabbing and oystering requires easy access to the water, thus the freeboard is low around the cockpit. Because the freeboard is low, gunwales are high to keep water out of the cockpit.

Figure 7. All of the boats in this photo are deadrises. Deadrises, like other boats, have designs that have developed in order to perform better and better in the conditions that they face. Very few deadrises look exactly alike and this is something that makes them interesting subjects for model making. Here are just a few.

Figure 8. In this shot of the cockpit, taken at the end of oyster dredging season, you can see the culling board straddling the motor box and dredge resting on it. The dredge is dragged along the bottom to pick up oysters. It is lifted over the culling board by a hydraulic winch, which is part of the mast and boom assembly. The dredge is emptied onto the culling board where oysters are culled by size and quality. Good oysters are packed into bushel baskets. What remains on the culling board is pushed over the edge back into the water.

Deadrises usually have a "skeg," which is essentially a fin that runs below the boat's keel. The **skeg** helps protect the propeller and rudder from impact damage, which is a common risk in shallow water. It also keeps the boat running in a straight line in the same way that the feathers of an arrow do, especially at low speeds.

Figure 11. A view of *ANNIE BUCK*'s beautiful bow looking down the ways.

Figure 9. Between seasons, when *ANNIE BUCK* is hauled out, we get an unusual opportunity to see the majority of her spacious cockpit without any gear in it. For spatial reference, consider that the motor box is 5' wide. The rear wall of the cabin is 11' wide and just over 6' high.

Figure 10. This image of the cockpit control station shows the steering wheel and throttle/shift control. The *ANNIE BUCK* has power steering. The black tubes under the stainless steel box are hydraulic lines for the steering mechanism. The thinner red lines are cables that run to the engine.

Figure 12. This shot of the underside, from the port stern, shows us a number of things. The bottom edges of the flared transom shows the relatively shallow angle of deadrise at the stern. This low amount of deadrise continues forward for a large portion of the hull, allowing for shallow draft. The skeg, which is like a large fin running beneath the boat's keel, is clearly visible, along with the propeller, rudder, and other components that make up her running gear. The large tube in the center of the waterline is the boat's exhaust pipe. The black oval shapes, just a bit higher, are scuppers, which are valves that let water out of the boat, but not in. Their location tells you the height of the floor inside, which should be even with the bottom edges of the scuppers to work correctly.

The *ANNIE BUCK* is shown crabbing in the late spring by working a "Trot line." A trot line is a long rope anchored on the seabed at both ends with bait secured at regular points along the line. A **roller** alongside the boat lifts the line as the boat passes, bringing up the bait and crabs, which are caught using a hand net. The hydraulically powered **winder** is used to bring in the line, which weighs hundreds of pounds when it is wet, along with anchors and floats.

Crabs are also caught in the Chesapeake using **crab pots** which are metal mesh traps. Pots are baited and dropped to the bottom. The crabs are able to enter the pot, but not exit. Each pot has a rope with a float attached to mark its position. Each waterman's floats are marked differently to identify the owner. The waterman checks his pots regularly, taking the crabs and replacing bait as needed. The way that crab pots work is similar to lobster pots, which are used in New England.

In the winter months, sometimes with temperatures in the 20s Fahrenheit, deadrises are used for harvesting oysters. This may be done by using **hand tongs**, which look like a couple of very toothy garden rakes with joined handles that are from 15' to 30' long. Using them means standing on the boat's deck and maneuvering these tongs to reach the bottom and haul in oysters that are at depths where they can't be seen. Other methods of harvesting oysters include using **Patent tongs**, which are larger hydraulically powered tongs or by towing a **dredge**. In both cases, a **mast and boom** are required to haul the extremely heavy loads into the boat.

Figure 13. The rear of the skeg and running gear. The running gear consists of the following: the propeller shaft; the propeller shaft strut, which supports the propeller shaft near the propeller to reduce vibration; the propeller; the rudder, which steers the boat and a keel extender, which connects the keel to the propeller shaft strut and the bottom of the rudder. The top of the skeg is cut away beneath the propeller shaft, which is unusual. Note that our designs were created before we were able to see this part of the boat and, as a result, our designs do not reflect this shape, which is an easy modification to make when building the model, itself.

Figure 14. This is a great shot for comparing how much of the length of a deadrise is devoted to its various areas. The vast majority is workspace. The cabin and pilothouse are far forward and the foredeck is relatively short. Freeboard is low for most of the length of the cockpit. Note the coaming (or gunwales), which surround the cockpit and become the walls of the cabin. Not only do they prevent water from washing into the cockpit, they form a connector between the hull and superstructure in both the real boat and in model construction.

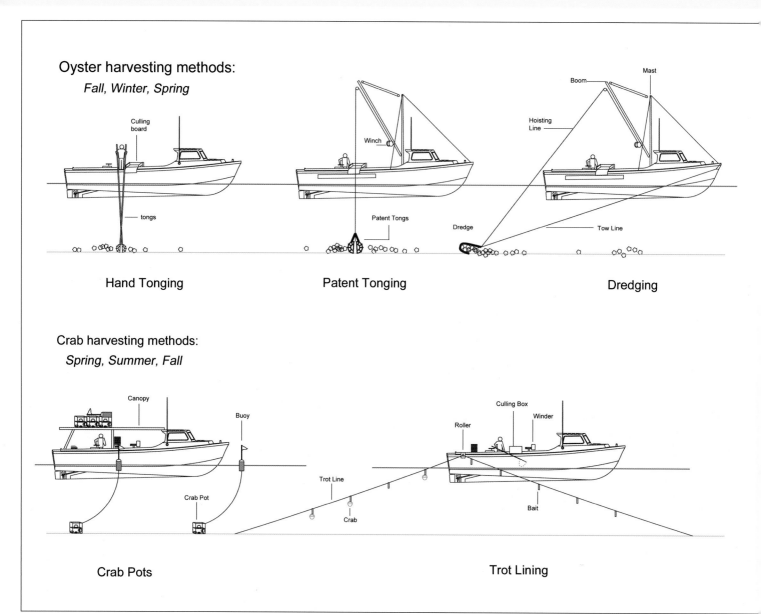

Oyster harvesting methods:
Fall, Winter, Spring

Culling board

tongs

Hand Tonging

Winch

Patent Tongs

Patent Tonging

Boom

Mast

Hoisting Line

Dredge

Tow Line

Dredging

Crab harvesting methods:
Spring, Summer, Fall

Canopy

Buoy

Crab Pot

Crab Pots

Culling Box

Roller

Winder

Trot Line

Crab

Bait

Trot Lining

Figure 15. This image shows some of the common ways that deadrises are used to harvest seafood, the winter months being the time that oysters are harvested and the summer months being the season of blue crabs.

Figure 16. Trot lining: If you look closely, you will see that David has a dip net. The line is being fed through a roller extending out from the starboard corner of the stern. The roller lifts the baited line up as the boat moves forward, bringing up crabs, which are netted and placed into the box in front of him for culling. You can see the importance of the location of the cockpit control box relative to where he must stand while he is working.

As with other deadrises, the *ANNIE BUCK* is used to harvest blue crabs in the summer. The Mid-Atlantic region is well known for its searing heat in late July and early August. In the mid-summer months she has a **canopy** for shade.

Workboats are built by boat builders. Until relatively recently all workboats were generally made by boat builders in the areas where they were used. Around here such names as Jones, Marshall, Parks, McQuay, Richardson, Lowrey, Kinnamon, Evans, Robbins, Mathews, Carmin, and others were and, in some cases still are, legendary boat building names. The boats that they designed and built became better and better for the tasks that they were needed for and thus there is a kind of evolution that occurred in their development. The *ANNIE BUCK* represents a relatively recent design in the evolution of deadrises and to truly see her is to understand her purpose within the parameters she works in. Information like this can really help you to envision the model you will be making in more ways than you might initially think.

The LOA of the average deadrise is between 20' and 45', although there are exceptions, both larger and smaller. The *ANNIE BUCK* has an LOA of 38' and a beam of 13'8". This means an LOA of 456" to a beam of 164". Dividing 456 by 164 gives us an LOA:Beam ratio of 2.78. The *ANNIE BUCK* is 2.78 times longer than she is wide. This information will come in handy in the next chapter.

Figure 17. ANNIE BUCK in her summer outfit. The canopy, which covers the entire cockpit, helps to reduce the heat of the sun during high crab season.

Chapter 12
Building a Three-View Drawing from a Tracing

We have been discussing all of the details that boats have, from the elements of the hull to the compound curvature of bow flare, and details, details, details. Do we have to make such a perfect shape? Do we have to make every piece of the boat in miniature? If not, am I really making a good model?

One of the reasons that I showed the hydraulic lines and cables underneath the steering box in Figure 10, in the chapter about the *ANNIE BUCK*, was to get you to pause for a moment and hopefully to ask yourself if it's critical to include each of these things. Whether you do or not is absolutely your choice and no one else's. Now that we have discussed all of the things that we have and we have discussed a lot, let's return to a discussion of the use of minimalism in a new way.

The *ANNIE BUCK*, like any boat, has thousands of parts in it. What is it that makes her the *ANNIE BUCK*? Your paper model may not be the fanciest model in the world, but when David first saw it from a distance, he said, "That's my boat!" There is nobody in the whole world more qualified to say that than he is. The version that he saw had no windows or graphics of any kind, but it caught him. It had the "essence."

That is what we should strive for anytime we begin to plan a model. What is it that makes the boat what it is and defines it from others? In the case of the paper model, I believe that we captured those elements of the boat that identify it despite the absence of others.

Bear in mind that this model was made with developable surfaces, so this model lacks the compound curvature of the sides of the *ANNIE BUCK*'s bow. What it does have, however, are a small number of important curves. These happen to be the major curves that we would put into in a 3-view drawing.

Creating a 3-view drawing of a boat is possible if you can get the right information. It is best to make drawings from known measurements, but that information is not always available. For a highly accurate model you could measure the boat directly. If that is not possible, or you want to make a simpler model, there is the possibility of making a drawing that starts with tracing. In order to do so, you must have a reasonably good broadside shot, as close to the center of the boat as possible and it should not be taken too close to the boat. You want to eliminate as much distortion as you can before you start.

We have such a shot of the *ANNIE BUCK*. From this photo we can make pretty good plans to work from for certain kinds of models. In this case, we are drawing these plans specifically for the purpose of making our first scratch-built model, which will be a "split-hull' waterline model.

We refer to this way of doing things as "by-eye," because we are not seeking perfection as much as we are concerned with being reasonably accurate, so that we can make a basic representative model. For a "by-eye" model, the more that we can capture of the essence of the boat, the better our model will be.

One of the most important lines for capturing the essence of any boat is its sheerline. It defines the tops of the hull and the edges of the deck. It can be very plain or extremely shapely. The chines pretty clearly say something about a boat, along with the waterline. Again, staying with the hull, the profile of the keel and transom are important. The outlines of the superstructure are also important. In the case of the *ANNIE BUCK* in particular, the way that the coaming runs around the cockpit and becomes the cabin walls as one piece that connects the front and the rear of the boat together, even though the front of the boat rises above the deck and the rear of the boat is primarily below the level of the deck are particularly important to us. These types of things are important to any boat's essence.

There are things that can be omitted. People don't generally notice the absence of a hinge, perhaps not even a steering wheel, if you catch the right things in the right way. You will develop your own ways of doing things with experience and again, what I see as a boat's essence may not be what you see and vice versa.

I do recommend that whatever your plans are, that you start with a good drawing. Making a 3-view drawing is not difficult, but it does involve making a lot of lines and you will have to look at the information available and make your own decisions about dimensional information that is incomplete.

Figure 2. This is a good broadside photo for making a tracing of the front profile of the *ANNIE BUCK*, because it was taken from a point very close to the center of the boat. Because of perspective distortion, a shot taken farther forward would cause the front part of the boat to seem larger and a shot taken rear of center would cause the rear part of the boat to seem larger. The resulting tracings would be distorted and, if used, would carry into your design, resulting in a model with a distorted shape.

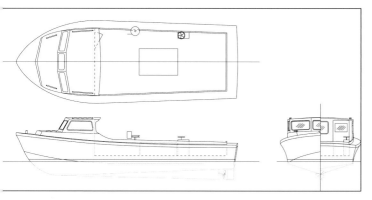

Figure 1. A large amount of the information in this 3-view drawing was obtained by tracings from the image below. Other information was added by "guesstimation," based on known facts about the boat and requirements of other boats of the type. The top view was made possible by knowing the boat's Beam:LOA ratio. Features below the waterline are fainter in this image, because they are somewhat more speculative, since we can't see what's underwater.

Figure 2. This is a good broadside photo for making a tracing of the front profile of the *ANNIE BUCK*, because it was taken from a point very close to the center of the boat.

Getting the best photo to work from is important, because it is the source of information for creating the front view, which will be an anchor view, as it would be with any other 3-view drawing. For this type of drawing, the front view will always refer to "broadside."

There are a number of ways to trace a photograph, either by hand, or using a computer. Make a copy of Figure 2 and trace along with the examples, using one of the methods outlined below, so that you get a good feel for it. It's not difficult.

Figure 3. This photo is not as good for tracing as the one in Figure 2, because it is somewhat forward of the mid-point of the boat, resulting in a more distorted image. One indicator that we are forward of center is the ability to see the middle windshield panel. Compare this to the previous image. The previous image does not give a clue that there are three panels to the windshield, so this photo does have certain informational value.

Figure 4. The blue tracing is the correct viewpoint. The red tracing results from the image in Figure 3.

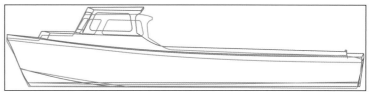

Figure 5. When the resulting tracings are overlaid, you can see that there is a considerable difference in their profiles. The red tracing, in this case, shows the boat as having less height and the length of the cabin/pilothouse area is too long. These differences are not terribly bad, but the more your photo deviates from being dead center, the greater the distortion will be in your drawing and the resulting model.

One method is to affix tracing paper or clear acetate such as is used for overhead projector images over your photograph. You will need a means of securing your tracing material and photo together until tracing is done. Masking tape is good for this. With tracing paper you can use a pencil, which is good because you can erase lines, if needed. Acetate will require the use of a pen. Acetate is good, because you can see the original image more clearly, but because you must use ink, you can't make as many mistakes. If tracing by hand, I recommend the use of a clear ruler and French curves to keep your lines smooth and clean.

It is possible to trace by attaching your tracing over a computer screen, but if you do, you cannot change the image size or location of the image on the computer monitor until your tracing is finished. We have done it and I will say that I prefer other methods.

If you do prefer to use a computer, you can scan your photo and then make your tracing with a paint program, if it allows you to work with separate layers. Assign the image to a lower layer than your tracings. One advantage of working with a computer is that you can assign different lines to different layers, allowing you to turn some layers off to reduce confusion without losing them, if you should want to refer back to them. Another advantage is that you can print

out copies of your drawing directly. If you trace manually, you will need to use a copy machine to print out your final product for the work of making the 3-view drawing.

It does not matter what size your tracing is. I recommend that you make the photograph as large as you can, beforehand, so you can see details more clearly. The final size of the tracing can be determined when it becomes time to turn it into a working drawing.

It is good to trace your photo in an organized sequence of tracings. In this way you can be sure not to miss anything. In the first tracing, you should catch the outline of the boat. In this case we want the waterline, the stem, the sheerline, the profile of the cabin and pilothouse continuing on to the coaming, the aft deck, and the lines of the transom. It is also a good time to capture the chine line. Note that the thick black curve along the sheer is not the actual sheer, but the boat's rub rail. Although it is visually more prominent, it is not the actual sheer line, which is just above it.

In the second tracing we capture lines that further define the shape of the boat and it's features. In Figure 7, we have now added the outlines of the cabin and pilothouse, the windows, the lines that distinguish the deck from the coaming, the secondary sheerline and the bootstripe, which is the top edge of the boat's protective bottom paint.

Figure 6. In the first tracing, we capture the boat's outline, the sheer line, chine line, and waterline. The result is shown below the photo for clarity.

In the third tracing we add in the small "other things" that may or may not be crucial to our model. We are referring to hardware, antennae, rails, graphics, various other gear, etc. It is better to include too much than to accidentally leave something out that might matter later on.

Figure 7. In the second tracing, we capture the lines that define the edges of the boat's structural features, such as the edges of the cabin and pilothouse, the secondary sheer line, where the deck and coaming meet, as well as the bootstripe. The lines taken in the first tracing are blue for clarity.

If you feel you have gotten everything traced that matters, you can separate the tracing from your photo and review it. This is a time to decide if everything looks correct and if all of the things that you traced in the third tracing are needed. Things that aren't can be removed.

Figure 8. The third tracing is the time to catch all of the other things. In some cases, you will want to trace things that may not be of actual value. If there is a question, it is better to include things of no value than to miss things that might turn out to be important later on. We have traced graphics, hardware, winder, trash barrel, David, culling box, exhaust pipe, and some other things.

Your drawing will form the front view of a working 3-view drawing. The process we use will require relatively few actual measurements, but there are some. Your drawing can be any size that you want, but it's not a bad idea to size your drawing to a scale, such as 1/2":1', or 1":1' as discussed in the chapter on mechanical drawings.

Although you may have a very beautiful front view drawing, we really need to make it more useful by making it 3-dimensional. The next step is to take this drawing and build it into a 3-view drawing that you can use as plans for a model.

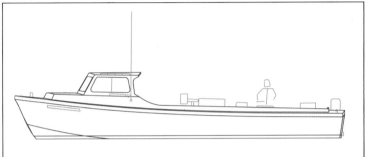

Figure 9. It is time to decide if anything needs to be changed or removed. We will eliminate a buoy from the rear deck, a box, the rubbish barrel, and, sorry, David.

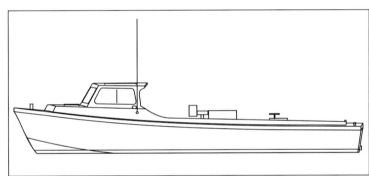

Figure 10. After eliminating lines from the tracing, we sharpen lines and edges where needed and end up with our final tracing of the *ANNIE BUCK*. I believe that if your drawing looks anything like this, you will be capturing her essence well, at least from the front view. I recommend that you make at least a few copies of your drawing and that that you put away the original tracing for safe keeping.

Creating a Workspace for Building a 3-View Drawing

If you are working on paper, you will need a drawing board and a T-square. You will also need a 45-degree angle template. (See Chapter 9, About Mechanical Drawings.) The T-square lets you make perfect horizontal lines. The 45-degree template lets you make both perfectly vertical and 45-degree lines. I also recommend French curves to make smooth curved lines and a clear ruler to make straight lines and to make the very few actual measurements that are involved in this drawing. Dividers are also good for transferring measurements without measuring.

If you use a computer, you can use the same paint program that you used already; CAD is even better if you have it.

Before you do any actual drawing, I recommend reading over this process beforehand so that you have a clear understanding before you start. The explanation may seem complex, but the process is actually pretty simple. Once you set up your workspace and understand how it works, you will find it to be a valuable tool.

You will find that there is relatively little actual measuring involved when your workspace is set up properly. All of the lines in the workspace have a role in making this possible.

The 45-degree transfer line is used to convey width measurements between the top and end views. Any width in the top view can be transferred to the end view by drawing a horizontal line from that point to the 45-degree line. Any horizontal line drawn from a point in the top view will cross the 45-degree transfer line exactly above the location of that same point in the end view and vice versa. We'll get back to this in a moment.

This is where the Beam:LOA ratio comes in. As you will recall, the Beam:LOA ratio is the relationship of length to width of the boat. The length of the boat is 38' or 456". The Beam is 13' 8" or 164". The formula for Beam:LOA ratio is Beam divided by LOA. 164 divided by 456 equals .36 (or 36%). It doesn't matter what size the drawing is; the beam of the boat in the drawing is .36 times whatever the length of the boat in the drawing is.

The upper line of the top view is a horizontal line equal to the beam of the boat in the drawing. To determine where to place it, measure the distance between the bow line and the stern line to get the LOA. Multiply the LOA by

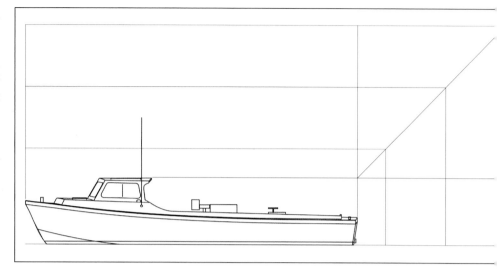

Figure 11. Workspace for developing top and end views to make a 3-view drawing. All lines are perfectly horizontal or vertical, except for the one in the upper right, which is drawn at 45 degrees. Lines should be light so that they don't interfere with the drawing itself. There are eleven lines in the workspace.

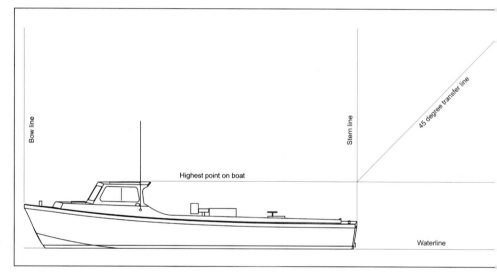

Figure 12. First, the front view drawing must be aligned so that the waterline is exactly horizontal. Next, vertical lines are run upwards from the tip of the bow and the rearmost point of the transom. Horizontal lines are made at the waterline and at the highest point of the structure of the boat. These four lines mark the outer extents of the boat's length and height. The lines marking length will be referred to as the bow line and the stern line. The lines marking its height are the waterline and the line marked the "highest point on boat." From the point where the highest point on boat line crosses the stern line, a line is made at 45 degrees up and to the right. We will refer to this line as the 45-degree transfer line. You will come to appreciate it.

.36, which is the *ANNIE BUCK*'s Beam:LOA ratio and place the horizontal line that represents the upper line of the top view. Extend that line to the 45 degree transfer line and where the two lines intersect, draw a vertical straight down to establish the rightmost extent of the end view. These lines, along with those already drawn, form the boundaries of the top and end views as seen in the blue shaded areas of Figure 15.

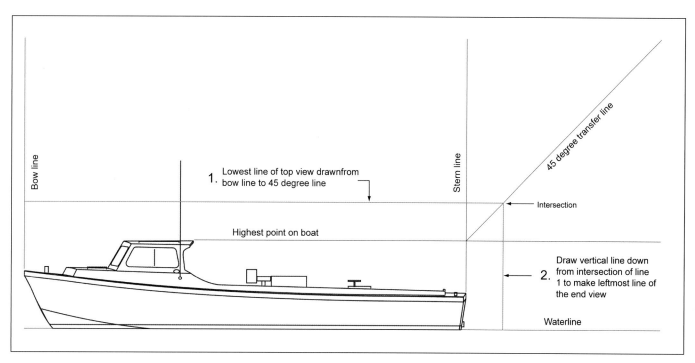

Figure 13. The lowest line of the top view is drawn as a horizontal line, leaving enough space between it and the highest point on boat line for clarity and note writing. The lowest line is drawn to the 45-degree transfer line. Where the lowest line and the 45-degree line intersect, a vertical line is drawn down to the waterline. This new line is the left line of what will be the end view.

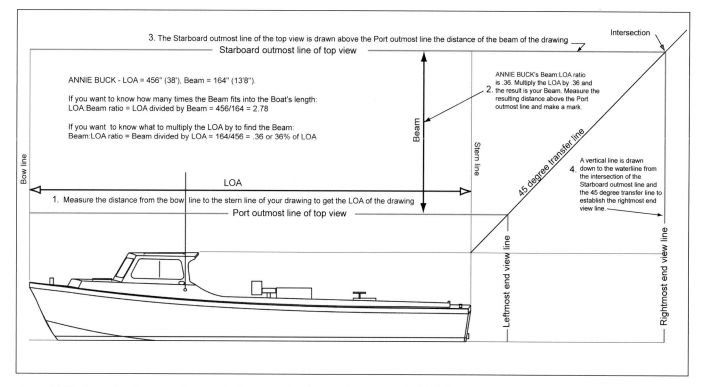

Figure 14. To determine the areas that contain the top and end views: 1. measure the LOA, 2. use the Beam:LOA ratio to determine Beam, 3. make the upper line in the top view the amount of the beam above the lower line, 4. draw a line down from where the upper line intersects the 45 degree transfer line.

As we have said repeatedly, the two straight lines that we know we can use to measure from the waterline and the centerline. The waterline is already established. Now that we have determined the containment boxes for our other views, we can add the centerlines, using a rule that will help you in many situations.

To find the center of any rectangle, draw lines from opposing diagonal corners. The point where they cross is the center of the rectangle.

A horizontal line that passes through the center of the rectangle in the top view becomes its centerline. Running this line to the 45-degree transfer line and running a vertical down provides the centerline for the end view.

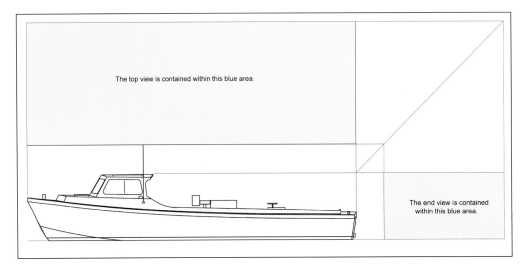

Figure 15. The blue shaded areas show you where the top and end views will be contained. The upper and lower lines of the top view are the width of the boat, as are the left and right lines of the end view.

This is how all of the basic lines of the workspace are set up and you can now make your own workspace. If you are working on paper and your front view is large, you might need to tape additional paper to what you have to accommodate the whole workspace.

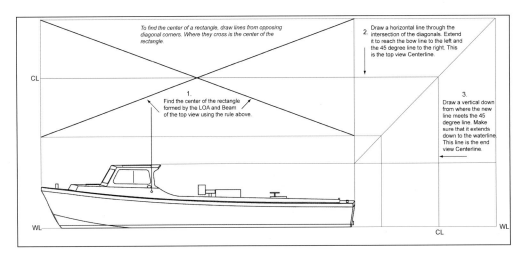

Figure 16. To establish the centerlines in your workspace: 1.draw diagonals, 2. draw a horizontal through the intersection to the 45-degree transfer line, 3. draw a vertical from where they intersect to make the centerline of the end view.

In the same way that we know, when we look at any complete 3-view drawing, that dimensions between the front and top views are carried over and that dimensions between the front and end views carry over, when we build a 3-view drawing, we can translate known points from one view to make them known in another. Because much of what we are creating is based on "guesstimation," having this ability helps to reduce the guessing part. In fact, by making transfer lines as shown in Figure 17, we have half of the information that we need to clearly establish the location of anything that is shown in the front view. For points in both the top and end views, the missing information has to do with widths as they pertain to the boat. This makes sense; we only have height and length information in the front view.

We are not totally without width information, because we have our Beam:LOA ratio, which is to say that we know the widest width of the boat. If you don't have that information about a particular boat, remember that you can look for examples of similar boats to see if you can find their LOA and Beam. Similar boats are likely to have fairly similar Beam:LOA ratios and if you have your front view tracing, you have an LOA to work from.

Other information will have to come from either known dimensional information, by making visual estimations, by thinking about what would make sense and what wouldn't and/or any other means that work. Because a boat is a combination of shapes that all fit together, the location of something may become apparent, based on how something else fit into the drawing. This is certainly where you will find some of the more interesting puzzles we've spoken about.

Pay particular attention to the Centerline of the boat. There are many things that you can see in the front view that you know are along the centerline. For example, the top line of the roof, the line that marks the center panel of the windshield, the upper and lower front tips of the cabin, the deck, the bow tip, the stem, the point where the chines meet the stem and the point where the stem meets the waterline. There are similar parts in the rear of the boat.

Just by running a vertical up from a centerline feature in the front view to where it crosses the centerline in the top view, gives you the placement of that point in the top view. The same is true for running a horizontal line from any centerline feature to the centerline in the end view. These are good dimensions and so the empty view areas are really not so empty, after all.

Transfers of information between the top and end views pertain to the boat's width dimensions, which is to say the dimensions that we are most lacking. If we can establish the width of a point in the top view, we can also establish it in the end view using our 45-degree transfer line. This is very powerful in terms of saving us work.

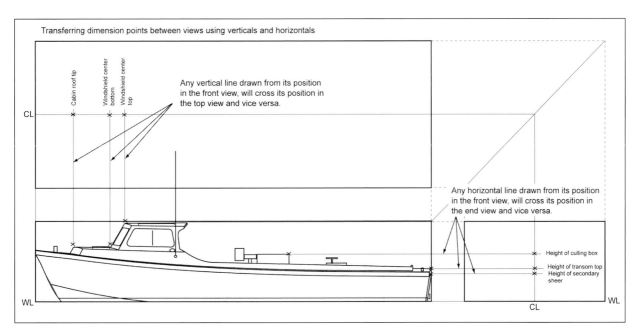

Figure 17. Given that we have a good front view, we know the locations of certain things. While our other views are starting out empty, it is not as if we don't have any information to work from. By drawing verticals up from points in the front view, we can determine where those points fall along the length of the boat in the top view. We can do the same for the end view to transfer heights from the front view by using horizontal lines.

Boxing allows you to transfer points between all three views. As we add our width dimensions into our workspace, we can compare between views and simultaneously fill information into both the top and end views.

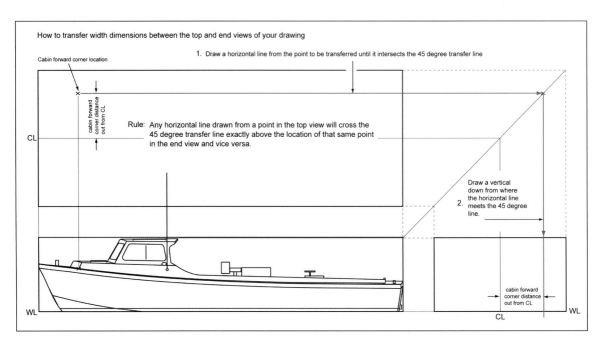

Figure 18. We can make this method of transfer many times more powerful by using it in conjunction with vertical and horizontal transfer lines from the front view, so that we create a box, resulting in a technique that I call "boxing."

This is a lot of Lines. I Need to Take a Deep Breath for a Moment...

Before we continue, I suggest that you leaf through the book and re-examine the various photos that you see of the *ANNIE BUCK* and the shapes that make her up. Pay attention to the amount of space allocated to different parts of the boat. As you do so, remember that deliberate planning went into the boat's layout in order to make her a good boat for the type of work a waterman needs her for. You will find that each time you look, you know her better. There could be something that you've thought about that doesn't seem to fit together until you look again to see how things interrelate.

It might also help to quickly review the chapter about the *ANNIE BUCK*. You don't have to be a Naval Architect to be able to learn to differentiate things that have an effect on a boat's capabilities. By the same token, you don't

have to be a waterman to figure out some of the things that would be good for a boat to have in order to make working on it better.

From here, I will give you just a couple of bits of information that I think might help and then you can take over and see what you get. Remember, practice will help you get better. If you don't like your initial results, try again.

Do not try to be perfect. It isn't possible using this method. Try to be as accurate as you can and you will do well. Don't forget that we are trying to capture the boat's essence. We are not trying to perform an exercise in geometry, we are trying to make something beautiful and a good drawing is needed to make a good model.

Filling in the Other Views

I believe that the sheerline is extremely powerful visually and the way it lies affects a lot of other things in the boat. In reverse that means that the location of other things can say something about where the sheerline lies.

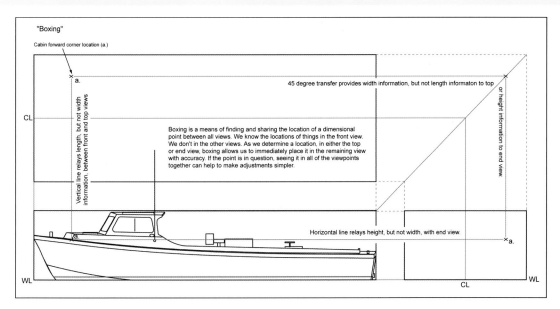

Figure 19. Boxing is a way of transferring points between all three views at the same time. We know, using a vertical drawn up from point a. in the front view, where it falls in the length of the top view. We also know, using a horizontal drawn across to the end view, what its height is in that view. Once we establish a width in either the top or end view, we know the exact placement of that point in all three views.

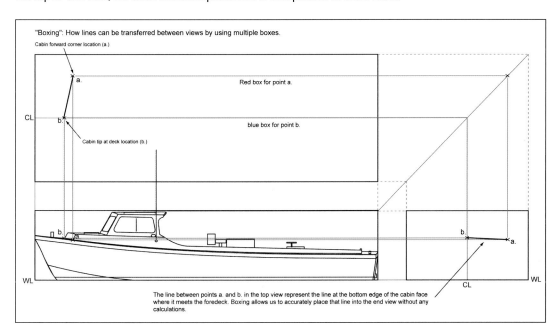

Figure 20. When we box a second point, in this case the bow tip at the deck level, we are able to make lines, which is the purpose of what we are doing here. The red line indicates the location of our original point: a. The point, b., is boxed with a blue line. When we connect the dots, we see the resulting line, which is the bottom front edge of the cabin. We can see whether or not our result looks correct in all views, so that we reduce the chances of making mistakes. Boxing lines should be light and easily erasable, because there will be a lot of them.

Remember that watermen use these types of boats for hand tonging. That means there must be some width to the deck or they couldn't stand on it.

I once had a boat builder tell me that most modern power boats have the widest point of their sheerline between the forward third and forward quarter of the boat. I believe that he is right in this case.

I would guesstimate that the angles of flare at the rear corners of the transom are pretty similar to the angle that

the transom slopes back at the top and that if you play with that idea, good things might happen.

If you find yourself totally stumped, check the various drawings in this book, including Figure 1 in this chapter, to see if taking just a few measurements from a drawing that works doesn't get you jump-started.

Good luck!

Chapter 13
Materials

There are all kinds of materials available to choose from when making a model and its various parts. Each type has its own pluses and minuses in respect to what you need it for. What you need to consider when choosing among them are factors such as sturdiness, workability within your resources, and the appearance they will have when finished. We can categorize the most commonly used materials as woods, plastics, and metals although, as we have seen, other materials and things that seem to be totally unrelated, when looked at from a modeler's perspective, can often be valuable.

We will mainly cover wood in this chapter. Wood is, by far, the medium that is used for most of the parts of the types of models covered in this book. Although wood is very familiar to us, because it is something that, in one form or another, surrounds us every day, there are some, perhaps unfamiliar, rules that need to be understood in order to effectively work with it.

Those who do the best work within any given medium are those who develop a "good feeling for the material". That is to say, that they consistently get the results that they want when working with it. We are only giving you some basics here, but there is an incredible amount of information to be found about all model making materials and what you can do with them in books, on the Internet, and to be gleaned by talking to experts who have experience working with them. I encourage you to experiment when you have a whim to see what possibilities a particular material may provide for you. It's through such experimentation that you can take things to higher levels.

Wood:

Throughout history, the dominant building material for the hulls and superstructures of boats has been wood. The same is true for model boats. The advent of iron, steel, aluminum, and fiberglass for major parts of boats is historically recent. Except in rare situations, wood can be used in models to replicate the look of all of these other materials, because it can accept almost any type of paint or finish. When making a model of a wooden boat with any type of varnish finish, there is no substitute for the real thing. Compared to other materials, wood is relatively inexpensive and widely available. It can be shaped with common hand and power tools. Separate pieces can be joined together with glues and/or fasteners. Thin pieces of wood can be bent relatively easily while retaining strength. When designed, constructed, and finished well, a model made primarily of wood can retain its structural integrity for years and years, as long as it is protected from harsh environmental conditions such as intense UV or moisture.

That said, converting raw wood into the shapes that you desire can be unexpectedly difficult unless you know a few things. For one, different species of wood have very different properties from each other. You probably already know Balsa wood and that it is different from most other woods, because of its light weight and how easily you can dent it or break small pieces of it. At the other end of the spectrum there are some species of hardwoods, referred to as "Ironwoods," that are so hard that a nail can't be driven into them and they are notorious for wearing tools down in short order. Such woods are used for special purposes, such as in the handles of fine knives.

Figure 1. You might not be used to seeing wood in this way. It shows the fibrous cells that make it up. They are similar to hairs, not only in appearance, but also in behavior. This is basswood that is rough cut and thin. Finished basswood is smooth with an almost imperceptible grain.

When deciding on the species of wood to use for a particular thing that you are making, you should plan to use a species whose properties best match the requirements needed for that thing. Those properties include appearance, strength, and other factors.

As important as the kind of wood that you use is an understanding that the flow of its grain determines how to best work with it. You cannot fully appreciate the potential of any piece of wood unless you know how to work with its grain. Doing household carpentry, you may find that when drilling or cutting with a power tool, the grain doesn't seem to have much effect on what you're doing. However, if you are making model-sized structures, trying to bend wood, or particularly when you are trying to carve wood, success depends on knowing how to work with its grain. The best place to start is to practice identifying the direction of the grain whenever you encounter a piece of wood.

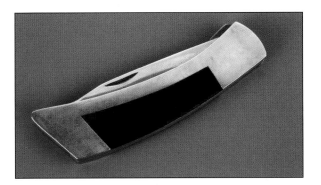

Figure 2. This knife is about 40 years old. The ironwood inlay is no more worn than the stainless steel that surrounds it.

Wood is composed of fibers that are tightly packed together. The lengthwise direction of these fibers is what we refer to as grain. When looking closely at the grain, although it appears to follow the long axis of a piece of wood, it doesn't do so perfectly, meaning that the grain often runs at an angle relative to the board's edge. It is not unusual, as in the case of wood flowing around a knot, for grain to reverse direction within a small distance along the edge of a board.

Figure 3. A really good way to see how grain runs is to find some old, decayed lumber of the sort in this photo. Some of the cells are gone, showing the alignment of those that remain. The piece of wood to the right has a hole in it. That hole once held a knot. You can see how the grain runs around that knot area and that it is not as straight as the grain in the other piece of wood.

Grain is important when creating a structure (additive construction). When making a part from wood, always align the grain with the part's longest dimension. This maximizes the strength of the part. When trying to break a piece of wood, it is far stronger when force is applied across the grain, which means breaking its fibers, than when force is applied in alignment with the grain, which is to split the fibers away from each other. Look at things around you that are made of wood, such as furniture or a door, and you will see that very few wooden objects do not follow this rule.

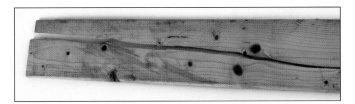

Figure 4. This sad piece of pine illustrates how line of the grain does not usually run parallel to the edge of the piece of wood. The split occurred as a separation between adjoining grain fibers. You can see, as in the previous image (Figure 3), that the fibers went around the knots, leaving bumps in those areas.

When joining separate pieces of wood, your connections are significantly stronger when there is an overlap, a spline, or it is, in some way, backed with another piece of wood. End grain to end grain joints have poor strength and are likely to fail eventually. Overlaps tend to make for good joints and are even better when the grains of adjoining wood run in opposing directions, when the situation allows.

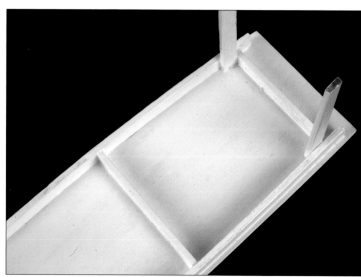

Figure 6. This is some of the joinery under a typical deadrise summer canopy. Note that the struts are tucked into corners, where they make surface contact with both the crosspieces and the lengthwise long pieces. Although a small joint, the surface contact strengthens all the pieces involved.

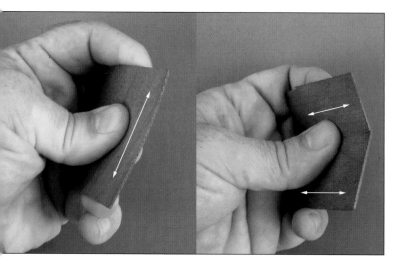

Figure 5. Both photos show the exact same piece of mahogany. The arrows show the direction of the wood grain. In the left frame, considerable force is being exerted and the wood responds by gently bending. In the right frame, almost no force is applied and the wood splits easily.

Fasteners such as nails and screws always cause some amount of damage to wood when used. The larger the fastener relative to the piece of wood it is used for, the greater the amount of damage, which can occur as a splitting along the wood's grain. This means that when connecting tiny model parts, such fasteners might do more damage than good and it may be preferable to use adhesives. When using fasteners, they must be chosen extremely carefully. Pins and wire are often the fasteners of choice and pilot holes should always be drilled before forcing them into place.

When it is necessary to bend strips of wood, you will find that certain species bend better than others and can usually be bent cold. Particularly good species for bending include Cherry and Ash. Others can be bent by boiling or steaming until pliable and then clamping around an object of the proper curvature. Some modelers like to soak their wood in ammonia as an alternative to boiling. All of the model types in this book can be made with cold bends.

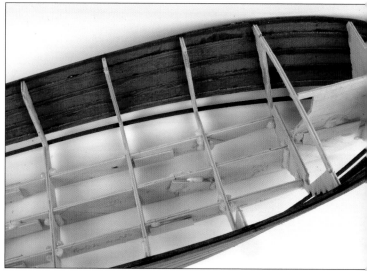

Figure 7. In this image of plank on bulkhead construction there are a number of types of joinery techniques used. Many pieces are notched to accommodate others. Some pieces are backed by small pieces of wood glued alongside them. The planks themselves are not only glued to the edges of the bulkheads, but to the faces of the long stringers that are aligned with the seams between the planks.

Grain is Important when Shaping Wood (Subtractive Construction)

Carving: the Epitome of Subtractive Construction

It needs to be said that before you even think about carving, any cutting tools you will use are sharp and in good condition. Make sure that the piece you are working on is held securely (see fixturing in the next chapter). We often work on a small section of a piece of wood large enough to provide a good handle and only separate the carved part after it is finished. This method works well for painting, too. Alternately clamp your work in an appropriate vise.

Just as there is a correct direction for aligning grain to the dimensions of any particular part, there is a correct direction for approaching grain with a cutting tool and going the wrong way will cause you to inflict "undue malice" upon the piece of wood that you are trying to shape. Basically, there are two directions that you can cut in: You can cut across the fibers of the grain or you can cut in between the fibers of the grain. Cutting between the grain is what you do when you split logs for a fireplace. It is not, however, a good way to cut small shavings away from a larger piece of wood, which is what you want to do when carving.

Carving, for the most part, involves cutting across the fibers of the wood to sever and remove parts of them. These cuts are made at an angle and are done in such a way as to cause the blade to simultaneously cut and pull the severed fibers away from the main piece of wood, regardless of whether your tool motion is made by pushing a chisel or pulling a drawknife. If you've ever whittled a small branch of wood with a jackknife, you can see what I mean. Despite the fact that you are pushing the knife away from you, the blade is pulling severed fibers away from the main piece of wood.

Whittling is simply carving successive chips away from the end of a stick. When cutting away from the end, your blade just lazily continues into space while your shaving falls to the ground. It's a comforting feeling, the knife smoothly cruising through your wood without resistance.

This is the way carving should feel! A good whittling stick is really built for cutting in the proper direction relative to the grain, because your blade is always approaching in a way that cuts across the grain and not into end grain, as in our log-splitting example.

As you also know, if you've done a lot of whittling, you keep the angle of your blade low, because the steeper angle that your blade has, the greater amount of force is necessary to make your cut. This is because the steeper angle results in your blade trying to remove a larger amount of wood, which also means severing a greater number of wood fibers.

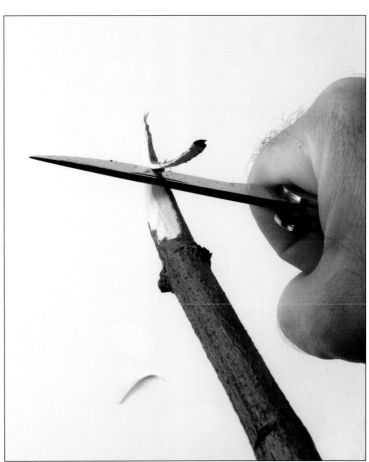

Figure 9. The rules that apply to whittling apply to carving; they just have to be applied differently.

Figure 8. This piece of walnut, which is 1/8" thick, has been boiled in water until pliable and then carefully clamped to a form, in this case a kitchen pot. When the piece dries, which might take several hours, it will stiffen to the new shape.

Wood planes operate on the same principle: they can be thought of as a wide chisel supported in a frame that keeps its blade at a good cutting angle relative to the wood it is cutting. It too works best when it is set to remove thin rather than thick shavings.

Figure 10. Using a chisel to carve.

The force required when whittling is also greater if you are not close enough to the end of your stick to remove it, because again, your blade would be trying to take a large shaving, this time as a result of the length of the cut being too long. If you want to carve into your stick, but not remove the end, you need to reduce the force necessary by using another type of cut called a "stop cut." A stop cut is used to sever grain fibers in order to prevent your regular cut from going past a certain point. Stop cuts are made perpendicular, or almost perpendicular into the wood. They don't have to be made deep. Shallow stop cuts should be alternated with shallow carving strokes until you reach the desired depth. Whenever you make a stop cut, your wood must be on a solid surface for support.

Figure 11. Using a spokeshave to carve.

In fact, your stop cut can be an approach from the opposite direction, as long as it doesn't cause you to cut between fibers. This gives you some versatility in the shapes you can create with your cuts.

Because a piece of lumber is really only a small portion of a large stick, with bark and considerable amounts of wood removed, there is a good chance that its grain does not follow its edges well. This means that if you simply use the dimensional edges of a piece of wood to guide your cutting, you may very well be directing your cut right into end grain, splitting the fibers of the wood. The result, if you apply enough force to cause separation, will be the removal of a chunk of wood, rather than the shaving that you intended. For this reason, unlike whittling, where your stick is the perfect package for shaving away, when you work with lumber you need to recognize how the grain fibers run so that your cuts will be across them and not between them.

Knowing how wonderful a cut made in the proper direction feels, the feeling of trying to make a cut in the wrong direction is one you will also get to know. Paying attention to this feeling will help you correct things before serious damage is done.

The act of cutting correctly, across the grain and down and away from the main body of your piece, is referred to as "Cutting Downhill" and is one of the most useful things to know if you are going to do a lot of work with wood. It is as important as knowing how to comb your hair. If you comb away from your head, you have a nice, neat head of hair. If you comb towards it, well...

The most important reason for learning to carve wood, for us as modelers, is that when we deal with wood at the size that we do, we can often do better to cut and shape things by hand with blades rather than saws. Cuts are cleaner and can be made very fast with practice. When making hulls or parts from solid blocks or laminates, as we do when we make split and lift-built hulls, it is important to carve in the right direction. The importance of cutting downhill is true for any hand-controlled blade that cuts as a knife blade would, including chisels, planes, spokeshaves, drawknives, jackknives, and others. We will look at some of these tools in Chapter 14.

These rules also apply when using power tools such as jointer-planers and routers. If you find that the surfaces you are getting after using these tools have small chunks broken out of them, you should examine your wood to see if you are feeding end grain into the blade.

It would not be difficult to write a few books, and there are many out there, on the various aspects of carving wood, but this is not what this book is for and so we need to move on. Once you start to have success with your carvings, you will find that it gets easier and with practice, you will be able to make more elaborate things. Remember, cut downhill, use stop cuts, make soft cuts, not too deep, too long, or at too steep an angle. Many light passes will give you far better results than trying to make a few large ones and will also take you less time in the long run. You know that you are carving properly when you have total control of your workpiece and over the behavior of your tools. If you don't feel that you have control, something is not correct. Some types of wood are easy to carve and some are definitely not. See below for more information.

One of the greatest things about carving is that you don't have lots of sawdust or noise and shavings are easy to sweep up.

Figure 14. The second cut is made at an angle to remove material. This piece of wood can be cut through with a knife using this technique properly.

Figure 12. A stop cut made as it would be done when whittling.

The following list of woods and their characteristics is by no means comprehensive, but will give you a starting point to get to know the characteristics of some of the more commonly available species of wood that can be used for model making.

Basswood and Tupelo are outstanding species for carving. Both are relatively soft woods with tight grain and creamy to yellow coloration. Their bending strength in thin pieces is fair to poor. They are excellent for making solid and laminated hulls, block-shaped parts, and for any pieces that involve hand shaping. Surfaces must be well sanded and prepared to avoid "fuzzing" when painted. You will see a lot of basswood in Chapter 15.

Pines, of which there are many species, are good general purpose woods that come from conifer trees. The available species of pine, because it grows everywhere, differ from place to place. Lumber referred to as 2 X 4s are almost always cut from some type of pine. It can be knotty, which is not good for model making, or clear, in which case it is extremely useful. Notably soft pines, such as Sugar Pine, are great for carving with a smooth soft texture, light yellow color, and tight grain. Redwood has a beautiful red color and is a great wood to consider when scaling down the appearance of Mahogany. Redwood is not easy to carve and can produce seriously long slivers – do not run your hand along the edge of a piece of Redwood. Some pines will retain an imprint of grain underneath paint, which may or may not be desirable for your purposes. Most clear pine is excellent for making long, thin structures, but are not very good for cold bending. Clear Pine is good for making solid and laminated hulls and parts that are block-, panel-, and strip-shaped. It takes virtually all paints well and is beautiful when varnished.

Figure 13. The first part of a "V" cut, using a stop cut. This downward stroke is the actual stop cut.

Cherry is one of our favorites when long, thin parts are needed and especially where bending is required. Its color runs from dark creamy to golden and it has a very tight grain. It is a moderately hard wood and is good for carving small pieces, such as grab rails, that would break if made from softer wood. It takes most paints well and is also beautiful when varnished. It is the wood that we prefer for making stringers for plank on bulkhead construction.

Figure 15. Pine.

Mahogany is legendary among marine woods. Antique & classic boats, the kind that have wooden planks with white seams and lots of chrome, are made of Mahogany. It is an absolutely beautiful wood and despite the fact that I like to scale down the grain of wood when I design models, I usually use Mahogany when making Mahogany boat models. Along with its visually beauty, its properties make it a wood that is used for internal structural parts as well. Although somewhat hard, it is not difficult to carve. It has good bending properties, as evidenced from its use in the side planking of boats. Of course, it is beautiful when varnished, which is why it is also used extensively for home furniture.

Figure 16. This shot of a plank on bulkhead model under construction reveals a potpourri of woods. The frame, floor, and bulkhead pieces are Baltic Birch plywood. The stringers, which are the long, thin pieces running between the bulkheads are Cherry. The darker wood that is seen between the stringers and as the rear deck planks is Mahogany. The wood that forms the decks, which is painted on the top is Basswood. You can't see it in this view, but this boat also has Balsa and aircraft plywood in it.

Teak is an extremely hard and dense wood used in boats for things that must take a lot of wear, such as decks and step-pads. Sometimes varnished when used as trim, it is just as often not finished. It is difficult to carve. It tends to be very expensive, making it impractical for making large parts. Unless you are experienced in working with Teak, you may want to substitute Mahogany, which has a fairly similar color and is significantly easier to work with.

Figure 17. Mahogany.

Balsa, which is used extensively for making model airplanes—in particular, because of its light weight, is somewhat less useful for making model boats. In model airplanes, Balsa is commonly used for stringers in wings and fuselages where it is covered with tissue paper. When making boats, however, the application of planks used in plank on bulkhead construction create an amount of force that balsa stringers cannot withstand and we prefer to use Cherry instead. It is also good for block shaped pieces and for some carvings, but does not carve as easily as Basswood or Tupelo do. Balsa is a good choice for making support blocks between parts that are situated at 90 degrees from each other to add strength within any wooden structure.

Figure 18. Balsa.

Special Plywood

Plywoods are composed of veneers of wood laminated together such that the grain of each layer runs perpendicular to its adjoining layer. This gives it tremendous strength for its dimensions. Because the fibers of each layer are in opposition, the rules of strength, where it is easier to cause a split between wood fibers than across them, are canceled out, since any attempt to break the wood would be across fibers.

Baltic Birch is a fine-grained plywood that comes in thicknesses that are good for rigid panels, such as keels, bulkheads, floors, some superstructure parts, and, occasionally, decks. When we make plank on bulkhead models, we usually use .125" thick Baltic Birch.

Aircraft Plywood is available as very thin sheets and is used for making actual airplanes. Despite being very thin, as thin as 1/64th of an inch, it is true plywood and, as a result, is very strong. It is particularly good for making the walls of superstructures and for thin roofs and trim. Because of its alternately biased layers, it can be bent along the axis of the grain, to make tubular and conical shapes.

As you work with different kinds of wood, you will develop your own favorites. Some of those favorites coming from the kinds of construction you like to use.

Figure 19. Aircraft plywood is very strong for its thickness. We will be using it in the construction of our split-hull model.

Plastics

The things that we refer to as plastics form a huge family of substances. What is available and useful for the boat modeler is a relatively small part of that family, but within that group of raw materials the potentials are amazing.

Clear plastics including acrylics, styrene and polycarbonates are useful for making window glass.

Other styrene materials, which are available as sheets, rods, tubes, girders, and other shapes can be cut and glued together with special plastic solvent glues.

For more advanced work, plastics of the class known as thermoplastics can be shaped with heat, some of which is done by bending with the aid of a heat gun. More advanced thermoplastic work is done via vacuforming, which is a process in which a heated plastic sheet is shaped over a form with the aid of vacuum suction.

Plexiglas or clear acrylic can be cut, drilled, machined, or turned in a lathe. The trick is to use the lowest speeds you can when working with it, because it melts at very low temperatures, clogging saw teeth, or making a molten mess around drill bits. Once your cutter is disabled by the molten plastic it is useless. It is amazing the difference you will see when you cut at low speed.

Plastic shapes can also be formed by making castings with plastic resins. To do so involves creating a master part, making a mold of that part using a material such as RTV silicone rubber, and then filling the mold with a liquid resin, which hardens in the mold to the shape of the original part.

Figure 20. The windows of *Happie* are styrene sandwiched between layers of aircraft plywood. Plastic is also used for the flag mast, just forward of the windshield. *Courtesy of Dan and Kathy Wilson.*

As you can see, there is a lot that can be done with plastics.

There are other things to know: Never let plastics burn as they release serious toxins. Plastic solvent glues are also toxic and require very good ventilation. Plastic solvent glues work by chemically melting adjoining surfaces temporarily to form a welded joint. Since other materials don't melt and harden in the same way, these adhesives can't join plastic to wood or plastic to metal. Super glues and epoxies are the best bet, but such joints between plastics and/or other materials tend not to be exceptionally sturdy. It is sometimes good to have a mechanical fastener, such as a pin, involved in such attachments. Also, some plastics, such as nylon, will not glue to themselves, or anything else, with any glue available to the home consumer. It's best to stick to types of plastics sold in hobby shops, because they are meant to work with available adhesives.

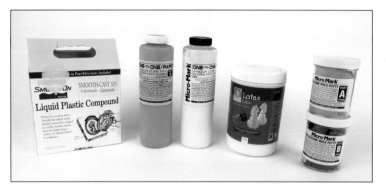

Figure 21. Some of the available products used for casting parts. From left to right, 2-part epoxy based casting plastic, 2-part RTV (Room Temperature Vulcanizing) silicone for making molds, paintable latex for making molds, and 2-part putty for mold making.

Metals

Unfortunately, we don't have the space to really get into metal here. We specialize in making custom metal parts and there is far too much to cover here. The good thing is that there is a tremendous wealth of information available about metalworking of all kinds at your library and the Internet, so please don't feel abandoned. We plan to write a future book on the subject of making metal hardware.

Other Substances

In the same way that we use different woods, based upon their different properties, adhesives have different properties that we can use to advantage and we should. Some glues are fast, but may not adhere to everything, or the joints made with them may lack the strength of glues that take longer to dry. Some glues are thin liquids, which require extremely smooth surfaces to make adequate contact, while others are thick, and in the case of foaming polyurethane glues, actually expand so that they hold well in cases where adjoining surfaces fit poorly. In other cases, we must be concerned with the glue having a negative visual effect on the finished model, as is the case with super glues that get on mahogany planking during glue-up.

Basically, for wood joints that require substantial strength, we tend to use type II carpenter's glues. For laminations and joints that are not tight for one reason or another, we use polyurethane glue. Both must be clamped for a period of time. The amount of time may depend upon the weather and the amount of glue being used.

Super glues are something that we use to join things together quickly. Some woods don't adhere well with superglue gels and not at all with liquids. You may have to do some experimenting. Super glues are good when joining non-wood items. One thing that has to be watched is that super glues cause what is called "gassing," which is a white haze that appears on dark and clear materials at some time after being used. This can cause a crisis if you use it to close up a pilothouse, such as the one on "Happie," because your windows might turn white and you cannot clean it up once the structure is closed up.

Paints & Finishes

I will only say a few things about paints and finishes in this book, but I think that they will help you tremendously, if you do not know them already. The types of paints that we use, when we can, are water based, which makes them easy to thin, using water, to maintain proper consistency during application.

One of the first things to know: you are not just brushing on color. You are also brushing on texture. Texture is a factor that is controlled by the quality and type of paint and brushes you are using, but perhaps even more than these things, it is controlled by how wet you keep your brush and the strokes you use. Use several light coats to get the finish you want. Trying too hard to get your model colored is what causes uneven areas, especially in terms of such things as permanent brush strokes, drips, and wrinkles. The color will come with patient application of subsequent coats and if your paint finish looks good, the color will too.

Figure 22. These are some of the adhesives that we use regularly in our work. Clockwise from top left: Type II carpenter's glue, Polyurethane foaming glue, high tack glue, 2-part epoxy, rubber cement, liquid super glue, low-strength double-sided tape, super glue gel, high-strength double-sided carpet tape, and watch crystal cement.

Before you can put on a good finish of paint, the substrate, which is to say the wood surface, must be ready. If it isn't smooth or if it's got fuzz, no amount of paint will fix it. I recommend filling, as we do with the split hull model of the *ANNIE BUCK*, and sanding to a grit of #320 to #400. Make sure that you remove dust with a slightly damp cloth.

Do not mix paints that use different solvents. Some paints, such as lacquers, use toluene, others use mineral spirits, and shellac based paints use denatured alcohol as their solvents. If you mix any of these classes of paints, your results, at best, will be a bad finish. At worst, you might cause a dangerous chemical mixture. This is why I am advocating that, for now, you use water-based paints.

Here are some things that you might want to know to get especially good results. You can polish paint, using very fine polishes made for plastics. You can varnish over paint once it has thoroughly dried. Bear in mind that some varnishes will cause yellowing, so test them first.

For finishing mahogany, or other darker woods, I recommend that you use polyurethane varnish of the type that has a mineral spirits solvent. Ventilate your finish area well, but don't have a fan blowing towards your work. Varnishes tend to set slowly and can pick up dust easily. The same rules apply to your substrate, except that you must use mineral spirit based putties. For the best advice on which to use, I recommend going to a store dedicated to selling paints.

More...

Graphics materials include a lot of different things that we can use as modelers, but two of the great ones are striping tape and rub-on lettering.

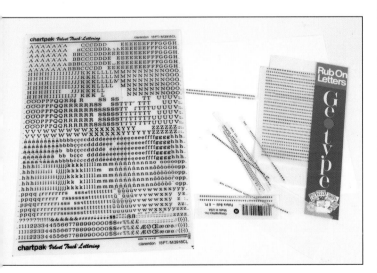

Figure 23. Rub on lettering is held over the surface that it will be applied to and the paper rubbed from the back to push the lettering onto the new surface. Its thickness is almost imperceptible.

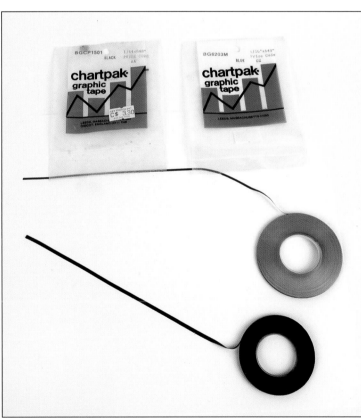

Figure 24. Striping tape has many uses. We will use it for our split-hull model in Chapter 15. It comes in many colors. It, along with some other graphics arts supplies, have gotten harder to find since home computers are now able to print out graphics at a level of quality previously only done by professionals.

Chapter 14
A Discussion About a Few Tools

We don't have the space in this book for a really good explanation of tools and their usage, but we'd like to touch on a few that are important to us. There are thousands of books on the subject, as well as books about how to set up your shop and all sorts of related technical information. Running any kind of good shop is something that requires the acquisition of knowledge and experience. If you are going to develop a workshop dedicated to making models, you will find that the types of models that you like to make will determine what tools work best for you, how you lay things out, and that you really cannot just go to a store and pick out everything to make for a good shop all at once. It is a process that happens over time.

I can tell you what tools I find work best for us and some things about them that I think are particularly useful for model makers. We have made models using almost every method that we know of and, as a result, have quite an array of tools. Our shop is inside an old boat-building shop and is probably larger than most people require. We have a lot of tools, large and small, and many odd tools that might only be used once and in the most unusual of situations.

When thinking about which tools are most important I find that there are some tools that get constant use and some tools that have barely ever been out of their original packaging. There are some tools that are inexpensive and easy to use whether you have a shop or not and there are some tools that weigh hundreds of pounds and make significant amounts of noise and dust. Some tools can be used for many different types of operations and some tools that can do only one thing. Some tools are those you would have in your home fix-it box and some tools are difficult to find.

Years ago, I walked into a barn in Vermont and was amazed at what I saw. It was a collection of farm implements made at the end of the 1800s into the early 1900s. There were threshers, mowers, hay baling equipment, and most of the kinds of equipment that we see on farms today. What was unusual about this collection of equipment was that none of it was designed to run with motors; everything

was horse or human powered. It was a collection of good working equipment, but it came to the marketplace just prior to, or at, the time that steam and gasoline motors revolutionized the farming, and other, industries. It made me realize that the current way of doing things did not always exist and that you can accomplish things using the often forgotten, but still valid, techniques of the past.

For any power tool that exists, there is a non-power version. For instance, the tool that we use most often for sawing wood is a 14" band saw. In fact, we use it so much that we have two of them. One is specially set up for "resawing," which for our purposes means to cut thin, flat material. The other is set up for general scrollwork, which means that it is capable of making curved cuts. Scroll cutting can be done by hand, the way it was done before the advent of band saws, using a coping saw.

The advantage of the band saw is that it is fast and accurate. It also weighs 150 lbs. and makes enough noise and dust to require hearing protection and a dust collection machine. A coping saw weighs a matter of ounces, could be used in your kitchen, and it doesn't cost very much. If you have the choice, the band saw is preferable, but if not the coping saw will do the job. A coping saw is good for scroll cutting. Unfortunately, it is not good for resawing. Any hand cutting of thin stock is a difficult matter and I don't recommend it. Resawing can be done carefully using a table saw with a featherboard if you have one. If not, I recommend working with a friend who has the equipment to make the required cuts or going to a woodworking shop and having them cut the stock you need. Also check hobby shops for precut sizes of wood to work from.

Table saws are good for many types of sawing, but can only make straight cuts with the use of a rip fence or mitre fence. Most table saws are unable to resaw wood wider than 3". The hand saws that would be used in place of a table saw would be a crosscut saw and the rip saw. Crosscutting means to cut across the grain, while ripping means to cut in alignment with the grain. Ripping saw blades, both hand and power, have larger spaces between their teeth, which keeps the teeth from getting clogged with sawdust—the main causes of burning wood and ruining blades. There are many types of saws with a variety of types of teeth that vary in their spacing, their shape, their sidewards angles and the metals that they are composed of. I've known woodworkers who have essentially made the study of different types of saws their life's work. For more information about saw blades check your local library and the Internet.

Scroll saws are excellent for cutting curves, but not as good for straight cuts. They are particularly good when you must make a cut within an enclosed area, meaning that you cannot lead into the cut from the outside. In such a case, you would drill a hole into your workpiece. You would then detach one end of the blade from the saw, feed it through the hole, reattach the blade, and make your cut. After the cut is made, you would detach the blade again to release your workpiece. This can also be done using a coping saw.

A drill press is another tool that we use frequently. Aside from being a power drill, the drill moves perfectly vertically,

giving control that cannot be achieved with hand power drills. In fact, I don't recommend using hand power drills because, for most aspects of model making, they are too powerful relative to the amount of control that you have.

A drill press can be used for tasks other than drilling, including sanding and light machining. There are several types of sanding and rasping drums, as well as, flap-sanding attachments that can help when shaping wood. There are also buffing tools made to fit drill presses for metal and plastic polishing work. In addition to standard drill bits, which cut from the center, there are brad point and Forstner bits, which are designed to make clean and flat-bottomed holes respectively. Very small drill bits, which are sized by gauge, rather than fractions, are something that we use extensively, especially in situations such as attaching hardware with pins. Such bits are very fragile and we usually use a "pin-vise" to hold them. Drilling with a pin vise involves turning the drill by hand, which provides excellent control.

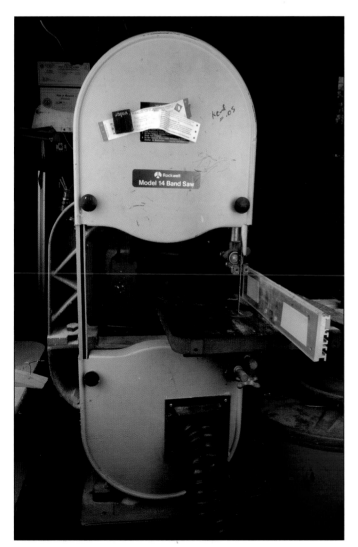

Figure 2. If you don't have a band saw, a coping saw can do much of its work, even if your shop is in an apartment building.

Figure 1. The workhorse of our shop is the band saw. It is an extremely versatile tool for our uses.

Flexible shaft tools are very good to have, especially those with foot controls. They can perform all of the functions of power drills, but with considerably greater control. With the various bits and attachments available for them, they are particularly good for final shaping of wood, plastic, and metal parts.

Before we continue on to other tools used for turning raw materials into what we need, I must hit on an area that our friend Irv enlightened us about. Irv is a machinist's machinist. He introduced me to the verb, to "fixture." Fixturing is not a foreign concept to anyone who works in a shop, although those that do it might not know that name for it. It may be a concept that doesn't get enough attention paid to it. As machinists know, fixturing is very important and doing it right, for some situations, can be a very difficult matter. Basically what I'm talking about now is how to correctly hold your workpiece to get the best results. This may not seem very important, but if you are going to make very delicate, small, fragile things, you will have to learn how to hold them in place carefully to work on them.

Fixturing in model making often means finding ways to secure your piece so that you have both hands free. For jobs that require significant force, such as sawing, carving or drilling, it is essential that your piece is held in a way that you can do the operation well, but also so it is held absolutely rigidly. This means understanding how to use vises and other holding techniques well. Sometimes it takes extra time to figure out the best method, but it will be worth it.

In other cases, fixturing means to make it easier to work on a piece or it means to increase the control you have over the piece that might otherwise be difficult to hold still. One way of increasing control over a very small carving is to make sure that you keep it attached to the larger piece of wood that it comes from until you are done carving it. In this way you are giving it a handle. There are also tools such as jeweler's vises and pin vises that are made specially for the purpose of securely holding small items.

Giving thought to fixturing in advance often helps to preempt problem situations. There are many, many tools for fixturing and it is another subject that you can research in your local library and on the Internet.

We do a lot of cutting that is not sawing. We often use thin materials, which we cut with a variety of knives and scissors. These materials may be fabric, paper, thin wood, and thin metal.

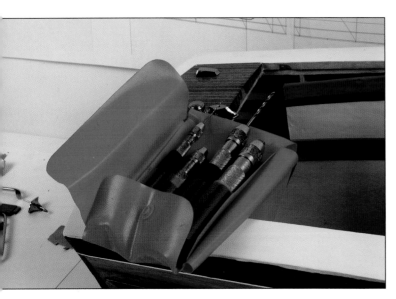

Figure 3. Pin vises, which we mainly use for turning drill bits precisely by hand, are also a type of fixturing device.

Figure 4. A collection of tools specifically designed for the various jobs of fixturing. If you don't tend to give fixturing much thought in your work, you might want to see how a more deliberate use of fixturing tools can help you get better results.

A plank on bulkhead model cannot be placed into a vise with jaws large enough to hold it without destroying it. When carving a piece of wood, it must be held rigidly in place, not only so that you that get good results, but much more importantly, so you don't have a terrible accident, because your workpiece shifted suddenly. Holding an object in one hand, in order to paint it using the other, especially if your hands shake, like mine do, could get the paint onto places that you don't want. The point is that; for whatever task you are doing, if your piece is not held well, your project or you could suffer.

Another type of cutting that we do extensively is carving. We have discussed some of the principles of carving in Chapter 13 and we will get back into them in Chapter 15. The tools involved are really types of knives, including those dedicated to carving, such as chisels and gouges, and those of the plane family including all types of planes, spokeshaves, and other tools with a single blade.

Figure 5. These are some of the most common single blade knife tools we use. Note the bevels, or angles of the cutting edges. Chisels and gouges have their cutting edges at the end of the tool. Knives have them on the side of the tool. Planes are basically chisels encased in a frame that controls their angle and depth. Note that some blades are beveled on one side, others on both.

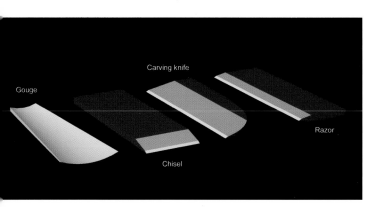

Figure 6. Typical types of blades for woodworking. They are the same as the four knives in the middle of Figure 7.

Carving knives are hand held and the cutting edge of the blade is on the side. Chisels have their cutting edge on the front of the blade. Gouges are chisels with arched cutting edges, for making concave cuts. Mallets are sometimes used with chisels and gouges in order to increase their cutting power. This is done on rare occasion with solid or lift-built models, but not for other types of model making.

Those of the plane family have a housing that is designed to hold the blade in a specific way relative to the wood being cut. This has to do with the results desired. Most tools that are referred to as planes are meant to achieve a smooth, oftentimes flat surface. The longer the bed, which is the bottom surface of the plane, the more it is meant to flatten large areas. Spokeshaves are meant to cut surfaces smooth, but allow for more contour in the finished piece. Their name was derived because they were used to shape the spokes of wagon wheels.

Figure 7. Removing wood with a straight chisel.

For thin wood and paper, we often use utility knives, single edge razor blades, and hobby knives. Sometimes these are used in conjunction with a cutting mat. These tools can make very precise cuts, but can dull quickly. Blade replacement is easy.

Figure 8. All of these tools, except for the top one, are types of planes. The top one is a drawknife, which, because it has no housing for the blade, is not a plane.

Clamps may seem like the same thing as fixturing tools, but they really aren't. You have probably heard the saying that "you can never have too many clamps around." I have to agree. There are many sizes and types of clamps. Spring clamps are useful for a variety of purposes, but any clamp that has a screw in its mechanism is stronger. Multiple clamps will give more hold.

Problems with clamps include marring surface finishes, clamping too hard, which cannot only break things, but can cause what is referred to as "glue starvation," by actually squeezing glue out of a joint, leaving the remaining glue insufficient for a good joint. It is always a good idea to test clamp any piece before using glue, to be sure that everything will work well in an actual glue-up. Note that until glue sets, it can act as a lubricant, allowing parts to shift from each other.

Sanding blocks are important, because they give sandpaper a rigid backing. If you've always sanded with your hands, you will find that, aside from the blisters you end up with, you have soft, poorly defined features to your work. When sanding, you are trying to change the shape, or at least the surface, of an object and it goes much better if there is an object behind the sandpaper. For instance, when trying to sand a concave shape into something, you will get better results with a sanding block that is round or cylindrical.

Some of our most important tools aren't considered by some be tools: clothespins, plastic cups, rubber bands, and many, many other things are tools for us. Keep your eyes open for items that can help you do what you need. A modeler's shop can be a very interesting place.

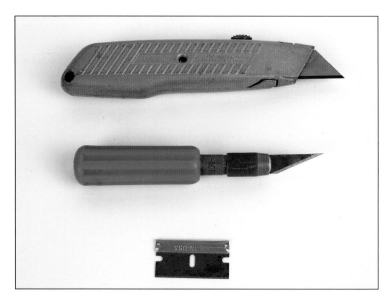

Figure 9. Knives of the razor family.

Figure 10. Nothing cuts thin materials more precisely than various razor knives with cutting mats.

Figure 11. Various types of clamps and clamping devices. On top are bar clamps. To the right are spring clamps. To the left are "C" clamps and in the middle are wooden screw clamps. Of great importance to us, as well, are the rubber bands and clothespin, also pictured.

Figure 12. Using a cylindrical sanding block to put a concave shape into the bottom of a pilothouse.

Figure 13. When rounding a convex surface, such as the crown of this cabin roof, you should use a flat or concave sanding block.

Chapter 15
Split-Hull Model Construction

Overview

If you made your own drawing in Chapter 12, this is a chance to see how a model made from it will come out. If not, we have plans here to work from. These plans are set up in a way to facilitate this method of model building and if you are using your own, you may want to note these modifications to use with yours. Whichever plans you use, once you've made this type of model, you will have a good understanding of a good way to make a model that most people don't know about.

The underlying principle behind model design, and in particular this type of model, is to convert the whole into a set of components or subassemblies. More specifically, I mean that we are looking at the shapes that make up the model and deconstructing them to a set of parts that can be worked on practically. When those parts are ready, we can put them together to build the whole.

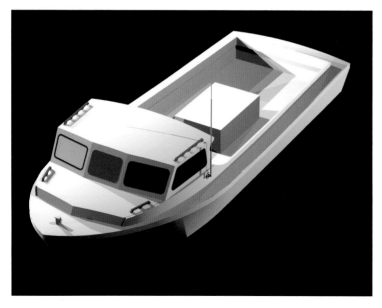

Figure 1.

Where the separations are made in deconstructing a model's shape are important, and different boats might call for separation along different lines. The sequence in which those parts are put together is as important as where parts are separated. Some parts may be installed as finished units while others have to be put together before finishing them, so that everything meshes between them.

For this model of the *ANNIE BUCK*, the separations are pretty straightforward and I think that you'll find that they make common sense. One of the important goals, whenever deciding where to make separations, is to plan in such a way that reduces difficult types of work.

Deconstructing the Hull

We have already spoken of different areas of a boat, including the hull, deck, and superstructure. For model construction we need to break these areas down further. For the *ANNIE BUCK*, the first dividing line of our deconstruction, looking from a front view, is to separate the superstructure from the hull along the sheerline. The coaming plays a particularly special role in the construction of this and many other kinds of boats. It is not part of the hull, but it isn't really superstructure either. For the moment, we will group it with the superstructure as we work on the hull.

This model is designed to be a waterline model, meaning that it is flat at the waterline and there is no hull structure below it. If later, you wish to add the rest of the hull, it's not hard. We'll discuss that option.

If you look at the block that forms the hull, there are many ways that you could construct it. One choice would be to try to carve it from one piece of wood. The outer shape would not be terribly difficult to cut with a saw and/or carve; however, trying to accurately carve out the area that makes up the cockpit cavity would require some pretty high level carving abilities, not to mention a good deal of unnecessary work.

Figure 2. Isolating the hull.

To make things easier, we do two things. First, we separate the portion behind the rear coaming to form what we call the **transom block**. We then separate the bottom portion of the hull at the level of the cockpit floor. We call the part below the floor line the **floor plate**. The remainder of the hull is split along the centerline, which is why we call it split-hull construction. These last two pieces mirror each other and we call these the **hull halves**. Thus, we have broken the hull into four parts: the transom block, the floor plate and port and starboard hull halves.

Separating the hull in this way means that no internal carving is necessary. Also, each of the four parts can be cut from rectangular blocks. Using double-sided carpet tape to attach our plans directly to these blocks, we can cut the rough shapes of these parts without having to make marks on the wood, which would require significant transfer of measurements and redrawing of lines.

Superstructure

Superstructure is an interesting thing in a model. I think that most model makers usually use basic superstructures when making models with hulls that aren't highly intricate and vice-versa. The fact of the matter is that superstructure and hull structure are totally independent of each other. This is to say that a split-hull model does not actually require any different superstructure than a plank on bulkhead model. A split-hull model can have an extremely detailed superstructure with clear windows and a full array of interior features within it and in some cases, since you are unable to see the internal structure of the hull, it could be assumed to be a plank on frame model.

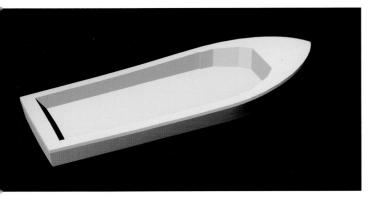

Figure 3. The hull alone.

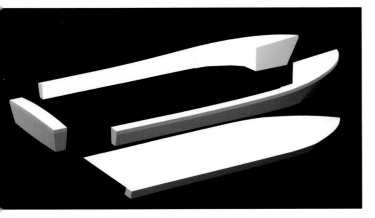

Figure 4. Separating the hull's shape into workable parts.

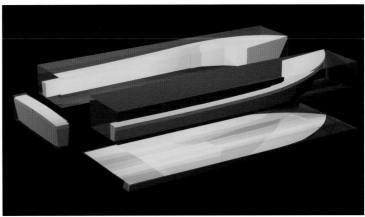

Figure 5. Here are the blocks that contain the four parts of the hull. These blocks are shown by blue lines on page 1 of the plans.

For this model of the *ANNIE BUCK*, we are keeping the superstructure simple using opaque windows. This means that our windows are printed or painted onto block structures. Factors in our choice include the relative ease with which we can shape solid blocks vs. the work of designing framework to support curved surfaces such as the cabin and pilothouse roofs. Another factor is that, if you are going to be able to see into the interior of the boat, there should be interior features to see and they require additional design. Again, what you want to include in your model is your choice.

In fact, the only modifications needed to make this model one with a visible interior are to switch from a solid block pilothouse to one that is made using additive construction, meaning that it is essentially a box made from panels. This means that the gingerbread would have holes for the windows, as would the three windshield panels and the bulkhead. Instead of the gingerbread being one layer, there should be three, the center layer having a larger area to accommodate the window. It is possible to use one layer and glue the window to the inside of the gingerbread directly, but you can see that glue from the opposite side of the pilothouse and if the window gets knocked into the boat, as they often do with this type of application, it is almost impossible to repair without serious surgery on the model.

Figure 6. *Ashley's Hope* is an interesting type of deadrise known by some as a "fan-tail;" the opposite type of stern from a draketail. She is a split-hull model and has a full hull and interior appointments. *Courtesy of James Wagner.*

We deliberately planned for the cabin block and interior lines of the hull halves to allow for an interior space to be made, if desired. If not needed, the hull halves could be solid from the bulkhead forward.

Therefore, you should understand that whatever method you use for building your hull structure does not determine the style of your superstructure, provided you design that hull structure in such a way that accommodates the needs of the superstructure. Those needs include not only interior space, if desired, but they must absolutely include means for the superstructure to be joined to the hull.

Figure 7. The windows of *Happie* are sandwiched between layers of aircraft plywood, which allows the model to have walls whose thickness is to the correct scale, while making the window installations very secure. *Courtesy of Dan and Kathy Wilson.*

Coamings

The side coamings of the *ANNIE BUCK* are what tie the superstructure to the hull. Starting at the stern and running to a point near the bow, they not only create a low wall that keeps water out of the cockpit area, but they also are the walls of the cabin. In the cockpit they go just a bit below the level of the deck, which is where we attach them to the hull in the rear portions of the boat. In the front of the boat, they hug the cabin block and you will see, that when the hull, the coaming, and cabin block are glued together, they form a very sturdy assembly.

The Rest

The components that we cover in this chapter make up the difficult parts of the model. After these assemblies are joined, how far you go will be your choice. You can make this a very detailed model or you may want to keep it simple. We will discuss some of your options at the end of the chapter.

Building the Model

The scale of the model, as shown in these plans, is 1/4":1'. You can change the scale of your model by changing the size of your copies. Bear in mind that this requires changing some dimensional information in the plans. I recommend that you make at least three copies of your plans. You will need two copies of page 1 to cut patterns from, the others are for safety and for taking measurements.

We used basswood and .040 aircraft plywood for all of the parts here. You can use clear soft pine instead of basswood, but basswood will be more forgiving when carving. Pay attention to the grain. Remember, the grain always runs in the direction of the longest dimension of the part.

First, cut the rectangles that surround the patterns for all of the basswood parts from their respective pages. I recommend using a utility knife and mat or backing board with a straightedge to make cuts cleanly and accurately.

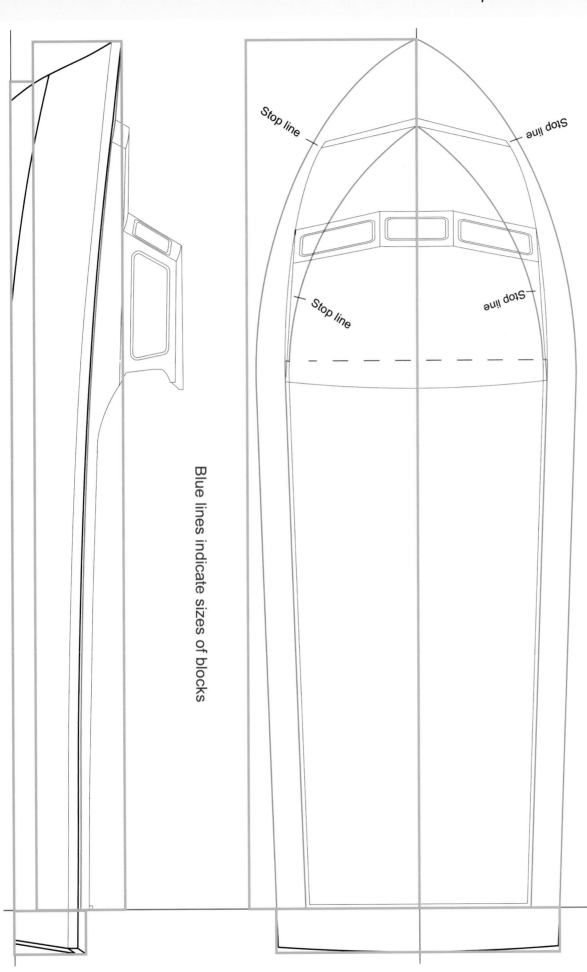

Blue lines indicate sizes of blocks

Stop line

Stop line

Stop line

Stop line

Figure 8. This is page 1 of our plans for the split-hull model of the *ANNIE BUCK* at 1/4":1' scale. It shows the top and front views of the hull. We are not concerned with superstructure on this page. The blue lines are what you use to measure the rectangular blocks that you will cut from. Red lines indicate sheer line and inner deck edge cuts. The grain of wood runs in the direction of the centerline for the hull-halves and the floor plate, but for the transom block, runs across the boat, which follows the rule of grain running in the long direction of the part.

Pilot House

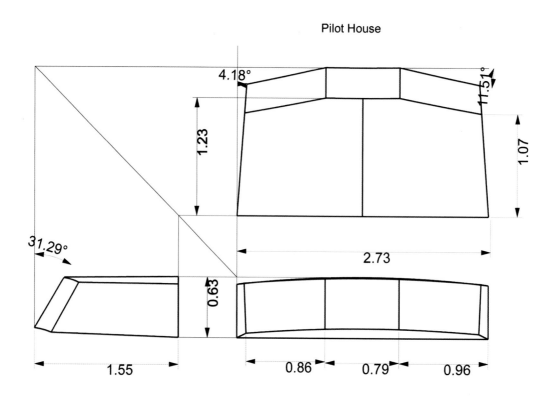

All parts on this page from Basswood

Line of Grain

Cabin

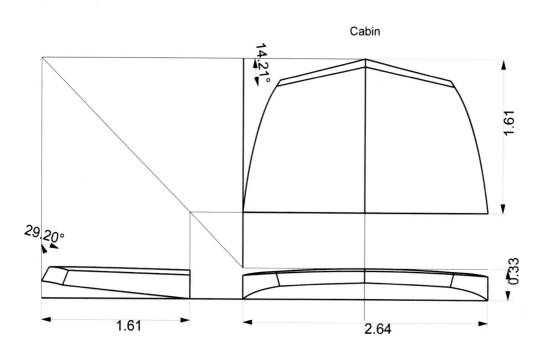

Figure 9. This is page 2 of our plans. It shows the plans, in 3-view format, of both the pilothouse and the cabin. Start by establishing rectangles that are the length and width of the parts, as seen from the top. Both your wood blocks and your patterns should be cut to these rectangles, which allows you to affix the pattern directly to your wood. If you do this correctly, you can ignore the dimensions on the paper, because you can simply cut through the lines in the same way as with the hull blocks.

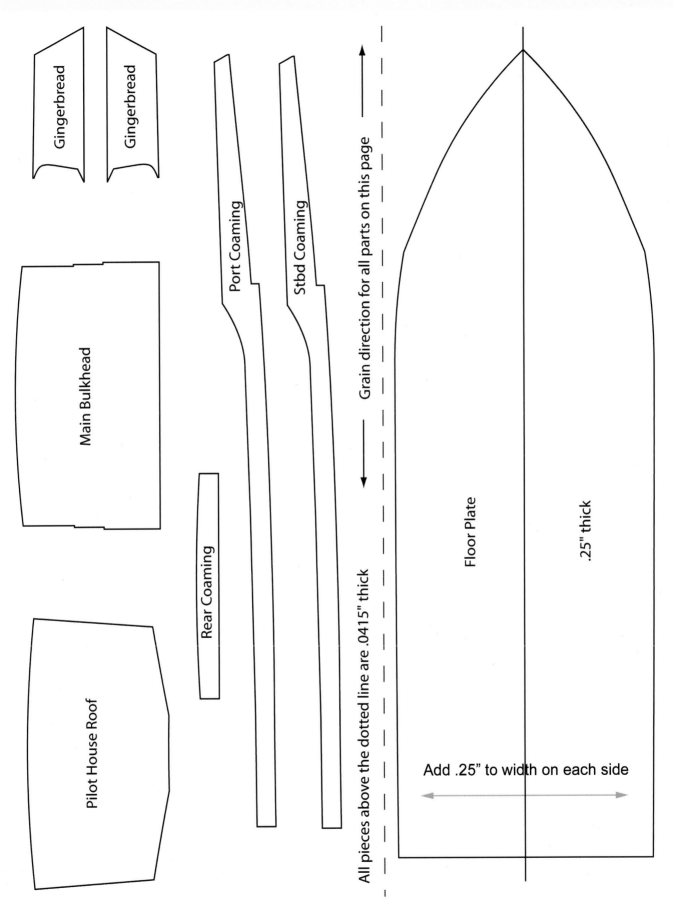

Figure 10. This is page 3 of our plans. The floor plate is shown on this sheet. As the notes indicate, cut a rectangle that fits the floor plate, but add .25" to each side beyond the width of the pattern. The reason for this will be clear later. Make it .25" thick. The other parts are to be cut from .040" aircraft plywood. Note how the parts are oriented to the grain line.

You should end up with the following blocks: 1. port hull half, 2. starboard hull half, 3. floor plate, 4. transom block, 5. cabin block, and 6. pilothouse block.

Figure 11. Cut each block to height, width, and length. If you are using a band or table saw, you can use your patterns to set your saw fence.

Apply the patterns to the starboard hull-half using the same methods. You will have to take the front view pattern from your second copy of page 1. Note that the same front view sheerline serves both blocks.

To maintain accuracy and, more importantly for safety, there is a specific order to the cuts of the hull-halves. The cuts are marked by red lines.

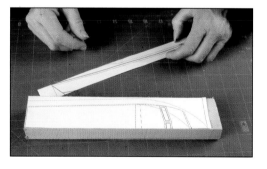

Figure 12. Using double-sided carpet tape, carefully attach the top port hull-half pattern to the top of its block so that the centerline lines up with the edge and the rear end of the pattern lines up with the rear of the block.

Figure 13. Using the same method, rotate the block and attach the side hull pattern so that the bottom edge of the pattern lines up with the bottom edge of the block and its rear end lines up with the rear end of the block.

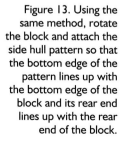

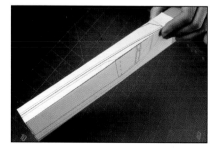

Figure 14. The first cut is the front view sheer line cut. Starting at the rear of the piece, stop at the point marked. Do not complete the cut or you will lose your top pattern.

Figure 15. The second cut is the inner line of the deck when viewed from the top. Again cut from the stern forward. Note that there is a slight jog in the line at the point where the bulkhead (dotted line) goes. Stop the cut at that point.

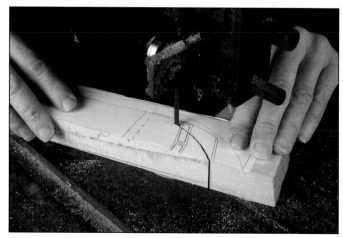

Figure 16. Restart the same cut from the front end and stop at the point marked.

Figure 17. The third cut starts at the rear and is the sheer line from the top. Again, stop the cut at the point marked.

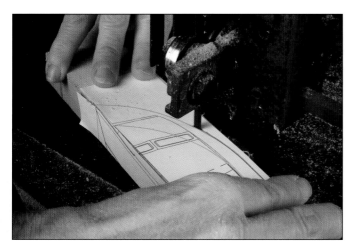

Figure 18. Once the top sheer line cut is made, you can complete the side sheer line and the interior cut. Finishing the side sheer line cut will sever the top pattern from the hull half and you will need to trace the top sheer line to the wood for cutting later.

Figure 19. Cut angle of the stem.

Cut the starboard hull-half the same way.

Now we get to the reason for not completing the top sheerline cuts. As you can see here, we are able to clamp this joint with a single small bar clamp. If we had completed the cuts, as many of us have learned the hard way, there would be no flat areas to clamp to and the amount of extra effort involved in gluing these pieces together can be staggering. For any of you who went ahead and finished those cuts, it will be a bit more difficult. I recommend trying large metal spring clamps.

Let the hull-half sub-assembly dry well. After that, you can finish the top sheerline cut. Sand or plane the top of the deck so that it is smooth.

Let's return to the other basswood blocks involved in the hull. Make sure that the top surface of the floor plate is as smooth as you will want it to be. One reason that we separated these parts was to give the model a clean look. Note that in this case we are making the floor the same color as the rest of the boat: white. If we wanted it to be a different color from the color of the rest of the boat, we might trace the interior of the hull halves onto the floor plate and paint it before we attach it. We would also paint the adjoining parts of the hull halves and bulkhead. By doing so, we wouldn't have to worry about masking or that our hands shake in order to get good clean separation

Figure 20. When you have both halves cut, remove all remains of the patterns and tape. Your parts should look like this.

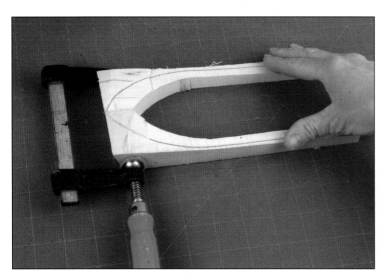

Figure 21. Using Type II carpenter's glue, we attach the bow center-line faces together and clamp, making certain that the bottoms of the pieces are aligned so that they sit flat on the surface of the table. As with any gluing operation, test your clamping without glue first, to make sure that everything will go smoothly.

Figure 22. After the glue has dried between the hull-halves, we glue it to the floor plate with Type II glue. Make sure that the bottom of the hull-halves assembly is flat: if not, sand the bottom to correct. The rear ends of the hull-halves must line up with the rear edge of the floor plate. Again, test your clamps first.

between colors.

If you have excess glue, do not try to remove it immediately. You will have better results with Type II glue if you wait 20 minutes, at which time you can remove it more cleanly with a sharp-cornered piece of scrap. Try it, you'll see.

When the glue has dried, the assembly of the hull, which was the additive part of its construction, is complete. Now it needs to be shaped. Here we will practice subtractive construction.

Figure 23. When this assembly is dry, use a sanding block to make sure that the rear of the hull-half/floor plate assembly is flush. Then, glue the transom block to the assembly and clamp together. The ends of the transom block should meet the corners of the hull-half sheer lines and the bottom of the transom block should be flush with the bottom of the floor plate. We prefer to use a single 12" bar clamp for this size of model. You will see that the semi-flat area made by our previous cutting of the stem line, shown in Figure 19, helps this clamping arrangement to work.

To carve it away, in practice for the more substantial shaping we must do, the first thing I do is fixture the workpiece. In this case I have it in a vise with a wood block that protects the floor of the cockpit, while transferring the holding power of the vise jaws.

The next thing that I do is locate the widest part of the boat—its beam. I recommend making a mark at that point. Based on the presumption that the grain of the wood is relatively well aligned with the centerline of the boat, I know that to be cutting downhill means to be cutting from that point down and towards the stern or from that point down and towards the bow.

Figure 24. First, remove the excess wood from the overlap of the floor plate. You can saw it away, or carve it away, as I prefer.

Figure 25. I am carving from the beam towards the stern. Notice which side of the chisel is up, the low angle, and the nice curl to the resulting shaving.

Figure 26. If I need a little extra power I can get it by tapping the chisel with a mallet. This one is designed for carving purposes. Be careful not cut into the transom block at this time!

Figure 27. Here you can actually see what we have been discussing about cutting so that the edge of the blade is actually pulling the fibers while it cuts them. The arrow shows the direction of the grain. Cutting downhill means toward the bow, since we are ahead of the beam of the boat. The line that the chisel is following is the desired cutting line. Because of the depth of the cut, determined by the height of the butt of the chisel, the wood above the line is splitting as it is removed, which is okay.

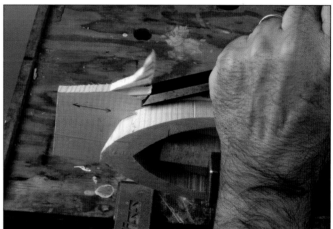

Figure 28. This cut follows the cut made in Figure 27. The top edge of the section being removed is the result of that cut. It is clean and under control because we are working with the grain. Since these are deep cuts, we use a mallet. As we get closer to the hull we only push the chisel by hand. I recommend practicing on other stock before making such deep cuts, but the principles at work here are those that guide the remainder of the carving of the hull.

We have only to remove the small part of the floor plate at the hull's stem. We can saw it off or remove it by carving a separating cut using a series of repeated stop cuts alternated with angled cuts.

Before actually attempting to shape the hull, it is important to realize that the grain of the transom block is in opposition to that of the rest of the hull and this fact requires careful consideration. If you hit the transom block with your chisel moving in the proper direction for the sides of the hull, especially if you are using a mallet, you are likely to break a chunk off of it. For the transom block we must treat it as a separate piece of wood with a different grain direction.

Figure 31. The floor plate pattern is used to determine the line that we carve to at the waterline. To put it in place, we must find the centerline of the boat. This requires finding and marking the midpoint of the transom and the center of the bow, which can be determined by running a line down the stem from the seam of the hull-halves. We then use a ruler or straightedge to mark the centerline under the hull.

Figure 29. A stop cut.

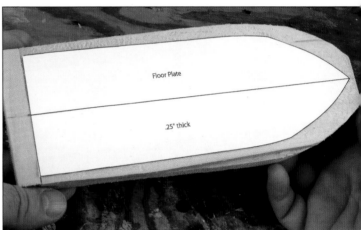

Figure 32. Cut the floor plate pattern from page 3 of the plans. Attach it with double-sided carpet tape so that its rear edge lines up with the seam between the transom block and floor plate and its centerline lines up with the centerline of the boat.

Figure 30. An angle cut to remove material.

Figure 33. Once in place, I usually trace the outline of the floor plate pattern onto the bottom of the floor plate, because I know that it might get a little beaten up during the shaping process. I also use a straightedge and continue the lines of the pattern to the stern. From where these lines meet the bottom edge of the transom, I draw a straight line on each side of the face of the transom up to where the secondary sheer line meets the transom. These lines represent the angles of the flare of the stern.

Now we can truly shape the hull; however, with this kind of model, things will be subjective. It is in the areas between the secondary sheerline, the chines, and the waterline that the compound curved form that we see when we look at the *ANNIE BUCK* really lies. I begin by removing material between the waterline and secondary sheerline so that I could almost lay a straightedge from one to the other. The result is similar to that of the developable hull of the paper model. After that, I add shape with a variety of tools.

From this point it's a matter of shaping the hull sides as you think that they should be based on the various photos and other information that you've seen. You don't have exact measurements to work from, so you are again working "by eye." I do the rest of the shaping with a combination of carving knives, and/or rasps and sanding blocks.

Figure 36. I love my spokeshave. Of all of the planes that I have, it is probably the one that gives me the most control in the greatest number of situations. When adjusted right, it makes beautiful curls. You can see here that we are carving a surface that runs from secondary sheer line to the waterline. A couple of points: we are behind the beam of the model, so we are carving towards the stern. There is a slight angle to the tool, my left hand ahead of my right. This technique is called "skewing" and what it means is that the angle of the tool is helping to slice as my hands move forward. Skewing is a technique that works for all cutting knives. Don't confuse it with slicing as you would a loaf of bread. There is no back and forth movement, just a careful angling of the blade during your forward stroke.

Figure 34. In order to prevent damage to the transom block, we saw away the parts of the transom that are endangered.

Figure 37. Remember to move towards the bow when ahead of the beam. Be patient, there are a lot of cuts to be made to get the right shape.

Figure 35. We need to mark the secondary sheer lines for both sides of the hull and the transom. We do this by setting a compass to the distance between the primary and secondary waterlines. We then run the compass carefully around the top edge of the hull to mark the curve of the secondary sheer line.

Figure 38. We don't want to get all of the way to the waterline in the area forward of the kink that tells us where the chine starts to rise. When your carving starts to look like this, it's time to change gears for a moment.

Figure 39. Using dividers, take the height of the front of the chines from the front view of the drawing and mark that height on the stem of your hull. Find the kink in the waterline that marks where the chines come in on the floor plate pattern and make a mark at that point. Do so for the other side of the hull as well.

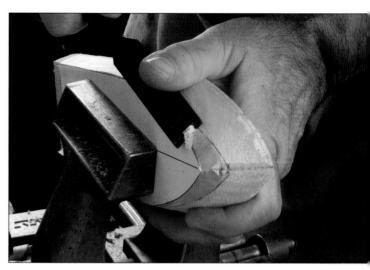

Figure 42. Cut the chines by using a straight chisel and light cuts so that its edge can touch both the chine line and waterline without any concavity. In this way you are using the chisel, not only to cut, but as a small straightedge to compare your cut to.

Figure 40. Using a flexible straightedge, such as a clear plastic ruler, set it on the side of the hull so that it passes through both the waterline/chine mark and the stem/chine mark and trace the resulting line.

Figure 43. Your chines should begin to look similar to these.

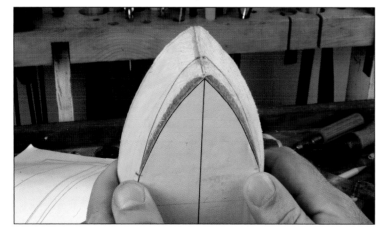

Figure 41. These lines are your chine lines and yours should resemble these. Fixture your hull in a vise with a block in the cockpit.

Figure 44. Shaping the face of transom is done initially with a chisel. Think of the line where the centerline crosses the transom as its high point. Working from the centerline out to the sides is how you cut downhill on the transom. Remember to check the dimensions of the transom against those in your drawing.

The Cabin and Pilothouse Blocks

We have two other basswood blocks to prepare: the cabin and the pilothouse. Using double-sided carpet tape, affix the top view patterns for each of these pieces to their respective blocks in the same way that we did with our hull-halves.

Figure 47. A small, shallow gouge can help to improve the shape of the stem where it meets the chines.

Figure 45. Here I use a rasp to add curvature to the bow and improve the shape of the stem.

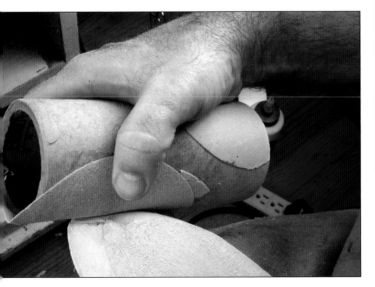

Figure 46. Using a homemade sanding cylinder to improve the surface left by the rasp.

Figure 48. Our hull is fairly well shaped and sanded. At this point we are ready to move on to the superstructure.

Figure 49. Cut the outlines of the pilothouse so that it looks like this.

Figure 51. Using a hobby knife, cut through the lines that mark the port and starboard windshield panels as shown. Remove these parts of the pattern as you cut them.

Figure 50. Using a straightedge, make a line from the line that represents the top edge of the starboard windshield panel to the bottom corner of that panel. Do the same for the port side.

Figure 52. The pilothouse should look like this.

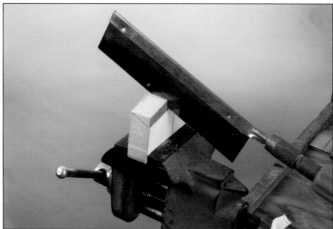

Figure 53. Fixturing the pilothouse securely, use a hobby saw to make a cut along the side edge of the windshield center panel at an angle and depth so that the blade just barely makes contact with the paper at the top and the bottom edge of the block as shown.

Cutting the Flat Parts

From this point on, things get a bit easier. For now, we will be cutting aircraft plywood. I prefer to cut it with a utility knife and mat, which I believe gives the highest quality of cut. Aircraft plywood can be cut with scissors, but this often leads to some shredded edges. If using scissors, I recommend only using them on straight cuts, not curves.

Figure 54. Cutting the faces of the windshield panels involves making a cut that runs through the angled line that you drew through the top and bottom outside corners of the panel and uses the edge of the paper to guide you. This is a tricky cut. Do it slowly. If it's not perfect it won't be a big problem. You can make some improvement later. Do this cut on the other side as well.

Figure 56. Cut the outlines of the cabin block so that it looks like this.

Figure 55. The center windshield panel cut runs parallel to the rear edge of the pilothouse, but is angled downward to the front edge. Note that the piece is fixtured by clamping to the workbench.

Whew! That's it for the pilothouse for the moment.

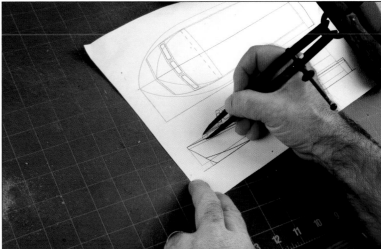

Figure 57. Because the cabin block has to conform to the sheer line of the boat, the bottom will need to be sanded to shape. The correct way to do this is to find the height of the top of the cabin above the deck and to transfer it to the cabin block from the top down, as seen in Figure 58.

Figure 58.

Figure 59. With a flat piece of heavy sandpaper, sand the bottom of your cabin block, with greater pressure on the front than the rear. You don't want to change the height of the rear edge. You want to change the front and you want the surface in between to gently curve.

Figure 60. Checking the bottom of the cabin block.

Figure 61. Using a hobby knife cut the front section of the pattern away as shown.

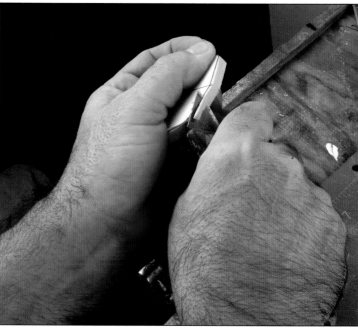

Figure 62. Because the grain runs along the centerline of the boat, cutting downhill means towards the center of the cabin front. Cut the front bevels using a utility knife with the paper as the top edge and the bottom of the pieces as the lower edge. Clean up with a sanding block as necessary. Be sure to do so for both sides.

Pay attention to the grain instructions. Small parts, like the gingerbread, will lose their fins if the grain runs in the wrong direction. Follow the same rules to cut all of the aircraft plywood pieces. Remove any patterns and any tape remaining on any parts of the boat. It is time to begin the process of turning your parts and subassemblies into a model.

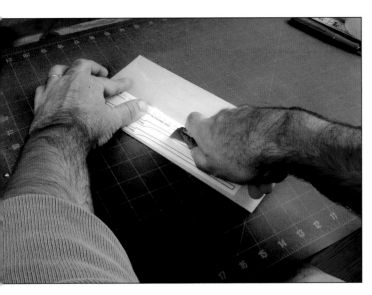

Figure 63. The coamings are small, but very important, so we need to take great care to get them correct. As with our blocks, the patterns are attached directly to our material, giving us good clear lines for cutting. There is some grain effect when cutting this way and it is best to cut using several light passes to avoid the grain of the wood redirecting your blade to a place that you don't expect. I recommend keeping the rear of your knife low on long cuts to get the best control.

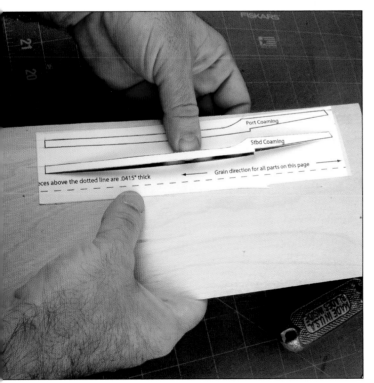

Figure 64. I make the most difficult cuts first. Difficult cuts tend to be the ones that put the most stress on wood. The greater the integrity is of the wood surrounding the area to be cut, the lower the likelihood of damaging anything while cutting. Also, I avoid cutting any one area completely free until other major cuts are made. For instance, I will make all of the long coaming cuts before making the short end cuts that release that part.

After the pilothouse is set, its roof must be crowned. This time there is a template to follow and that is formed by the curve at the top of the bulkhead. Now that you have some carving and shaping under your belt, I'll let you choose the tools to deal with this crown. The pilothouse roof must fair to it and it must make good contact with the top edges of the gingerbread, especially in the rear where the fins are.

Figure 65. How the coaming, hull, and superstructure parts fit together is critical. There is no model if everything doesn't come together harmoniously. Use small clamps to hold things so that you can see that they fit together as you expect them to. Put the coamings into place, with the bulkhead at the position already established by the jog in the top sheer line of the hull halves (remember them from Figure 15?). If the bulkhead is narrow, it's not a big problem. If it's wide, you will need to cut it down. The coamings need to make contact with the foredeck at the front while in place in the rear.

Figure 66. When you are ready to proceed, it is time to glue the coamings in. The bulkhead can come back out. It can be reinserted later by bending it to make it narrow. Use a minimum of three small clamps to hold each coaming in position and you must be certain that you like their positions. When you glue them into place with super glue gel, you will be peeling the coaming away in the rear of the cockpit, while the other two clamps hold the rest of it.

Figure 67. Because of the tenacity of super glue you will not be able to change the position of this piece easily. Hold the joint until it sets, then you can remove the other clamps and glue the rest of the coaming up to the bulkhead line. Do the same for both side coamings.

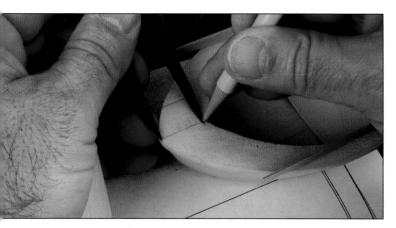

Figure 68. Transfer the distance from the tip of the bow to the bottom tip of the coaming from the top view of the drawing to the model's foredeck. Make a mark.

Figure 69. Place the cabin block on the foredeck so that its tip is at the mark you just made and visually line it up. Squeeze the coamings around it and decide if you have it in the right place and alignment. When you are satisfied, hold it in position and trace its position on the foredeck. The resulting line does two things. It gives you the proper position for the cabin block during gluing and it also leaves an outline of where you can safely put glue. Apply super glue gel within the lines traced and carefully put the cabin block in place. Hold until set.

Figure 70. Are your fingers feeling strong? Doing each side separately, apply super glue gel to the inside of the coaming, making sure it goes all of the way to the front of the part, put in place and hold until set. I have found that there is not a clamp that can do the job as well as holding it yourself. Be sure that the joint is good before you release it and be sure not to glue yourself to the boat. Do this for the other coaming as well. Take a rest for a moment.

Figure 71. We can now return to some simple carving in order to round the top of the cabin to give it its crown. This is done with a couple of easy strokes of a utility knife to each side. The curved shape is refined using a sanding block.

Figure 72. The next step is to reinforce the bulkhead installation by adding in two thin strips of wood on each side. Balsa is ideal, but basswood can also be used. The strip used is approximately .10" square. The first strips are glued in place with super glue gel along the bulkhead line inside hull and coaming. They are cut off with a straightedge razor at the top of the coaming.

Figure 73. The second pair of strips is glued along the inside top edge of the coaming. Both are sanded flush to the top edge of the coaming with a sanding block. This is how they look with the bulkhead in place.

Figure 74. Holding the bulkhead in its proper location, we let a small amount of super glue liquid flow into the areas on each side where the inside of the bulkhead makes contact with the new vertical strips. Hold it until the glue sets. The addition of these strips makes for a very strong joint by increasing surface area between the hull and bulkhead. This is the only time that we use liquid super glue on this project.

Figure 75. The pilothouse must be given shape, but before that, the gingerbread must be properly located and installed. The rear ends of the gingerbread pieces should be equally offset behind the rear face of the pilothouse block. This is because of the tricky nature of the windshield panel cuts, which might not be exactly even. Properly locating the gingerbread pieces by setting them to the rear means that we can use them to help adjust our windshield panels, if they need it, or to get excited about how good a job we did cutting them, if they don't. Their bottom edges must be aligned with the bottom of the pilothouse block. Before you glue, mark their correct location. Glue them into place with super glue gel. Since the front edges of the gingerbread are known to be at the correct angles, they can be used as guides to make adjustments of the windshield panels, which can be done by shaving small amounts off, where a panel bulges, or by building up with putty later on.

Figure 76. After the gingerbread is secure, the bottom of the pilothouse is sanded to match the crown of the cabin roof. This is done with a rounded sanding block with heavy grit sandpaper. This means putting the greatest pressure in the area of the centerline of the pilothouse. Be careful not to damage the gingerbread pieces from the sandpaper or from accidentally putting too much pressure on them when holding it.

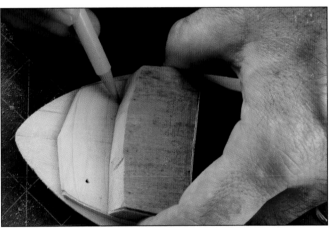

Figure 77. Test your curvature frequently by putting the pilothouse in place. When done, the pilothouse should rest comfortably in place with the gingerbread on both sides making good contact with the coamings. When the pilothouse fits into place properly, trace its outline on the top of the cabin roof, as well as along the bottoms of the gingerbread over the coamings.

Figure 78. Apply super glue gel to the cabin roof within your lines, the stripping along the coaming, and the top part of the bulkhead where the rear of the pilothouse will make contact. Now install the pilothouse.

The *ANNIE BUCK* is a fiberglass boat. Knowing this from the outset, we also knew that we would be doing a water based putty overlay and this meant that our tolerance for error was wide. When we do a putty overlay, we are covering the entire exterior of the hull with a thin layer of putty, which fills minor gaps and uneven areas. This is not the main reason for using it. The main reason for using it is that it puts a layer of smooth material over the wood, which helps to make it look more like a material like fiberglass.

Figure 80. One more piece completes the boat proper: the little piece of coaming at the rear of the cockpit. I think that you can handle its installation.

Figure 79. When you are ready, apply super glue gel to the entire top of the pilothouse block and the tops of the gingerbread and install the roof, being sure that you have it aligned properly. Hold the side edges tight until you know they are secure.

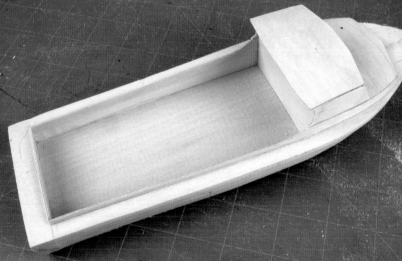

Figure 81. This is our model of the ANNIE BUCK so far.

Making the Motor Box

The motor box is made very simply, using additive construction. Actually, we have choices; a box such as this could simply be cut from a block. The simplicity of the construction of this motor box, which is basically the same type of construction that you would use if you were making a pilothouse that you could see into, merits an explanation.

There is a reason that you can't find plans. They are hidden in the paper model plans from Chapter 6. Since it is a model of the same scale, we simply took the plans for the motor box from those plans and cut it up to give us panels for this motor box. We did expand the top of it a bit. We did the same thing for the door. The door for the paper model makes a good pattern for making a door from aircraft plywood.

Back to the subject at hand. There are five pieces of aircraft plywood and some balsa strip, the same as we used to back up the bulkhead. The largest piece is the top and it is the last piece to go on.

Attaching the motorbox to the floor is done with a few drops of super glue gel. The door can be attached in the same way, or with double-sided carpet tape.

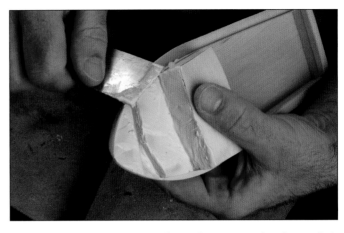

Figure 83. A putty knife or other flat rigid or semi-rigid tool is needed to force firm putty into gaps properly. It is also used for making smooth flat surfaces, as we would be doing to fix indentations. It helps to keep the face of the knife lubricated with water.

Figure 84. After filling gaps with the putty knife, we essentially "paint" the boat with very liquefied putty using our fingers. You can use a stiff paintbrush, but I find that it is good to be able to feel the depth of the putty as I move along.

Figure 82. Water based putty can be thinned with water. We put it in a container so that some remains thick, some becomes almost watery and what is in between varies in its consistency. We keep a small amount of water available to add when necessary.

Figure 85. Certain tight areas might call for the creation of small makeshift application tools, such as this piece of wood with a 45-degree angle cut into it.

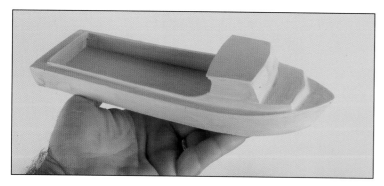

Figure 86. Puttying is not meant to take the place of good workmanship and can't be used for all, or even that many, boats. We don't want to leave a lot of putty on the boat. It will have to be sanded down afterwards and lumps could cause problems. Also, we tried to avoid using putty inside the cockpit. The difficulty of removing it would not have been worth the trouble. This is the amount that we left on the model to dry.

Figure 87. The next day, we sanded the putty smooth with #320 grit sandpaper and this is the result.

box, a crabbing net, or other things related to crab season. Or, we could set it up for oystering season with mast and boom and rigging. The possibilities are infinite.

Look at Figure 6 and you will see another split hull model that is both full-hulled and has an interior. You need three pieces of wood to make this a full-hulled model. The first is a skeg piece, which is the width of the skeg and from the front view, has its profile. The other two pieces match each other and go on either side of the skeg. They have to be carved to shape and you need to figure out where the chine line is, but we just did a lot more figuring out with the *ANNIE BUCK.*

Figure 88. Each of the two sidepieces of the motor box is lined on three sides with strips of balsa, which are attached with super glue gel as shown. They are sanded flush with the edges of the aircraft plywood. The balsa is easily trimmed with a single edge razor blade.

We are going to leave this model for now. I think that at this point, whether you used our plans or yours, you can get a sense of the process of seeing a boat that you would like to model and knowing that there is a way that you can do it. You have to go through the three stages that we discussed in the beginning of the book.

Of course, this is a relatively simple model as it is. I'm not saying easy to make. Even this model can be made considerably more detailed. You can add graphics, using rub on lettering, or things that you can print with a computer printer. If you have metal working skills, or the desire to experiment, you can make hardware parts. As I've said before, "metal parts" don't even have to be made of metal. This is just the beginning of what you can do with this design, though.

If we were to finish off this model, we would add grab rails, exhaust pipe, scuppers, name logo, and hardware, such as the bollard on the bow. We might also outfit it for the work it might be doing with such things as winder, culling

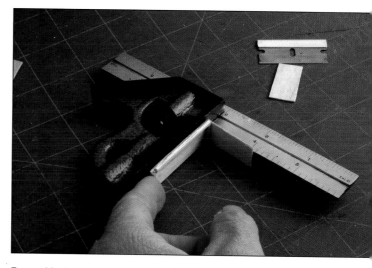

Figure 89. Attach an end piece to the outside corner of one of the prepared sides using a square so that it is aligned properly. Glue with super glue gel. Use the same technique to glue the other end piece to the same sidepiece.

If you think about the cabin/pilothouse arrangement that we just built, we could have made some relatively minor changes to our design that would allow for an interior. Look at both Figure 6 and Figure 7 and you will see that windows were installed by sandwiching them between two layers of aircraft plywood. There is no reason that the gingerbread of the ANNIE BUCK could not be similarly arranged. Of course, the 3 panel windshield would have to be designed and it might be a little tricky, but not impossible. Such arrangements can be put together with construction similar to the motor box we just made. Again, we would have to work out a way to sandwich windows and door into the bulkhead, but in this problem there lies an exciting thought. You could make a door that opens. The trick: ribbon sandwiched in the wall and sandwiched in the door to form an almost invisible hinge. It's not a new trick, but it is a good one.

The fact of the matter is, now that you know you can make a model, it's time to realize that you can take your skill to great new heights.

Figure 90. Both ends glued to the first wall of the motor box.

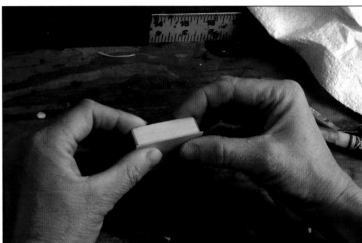

Figure 92. The edges of the sidepieces with the balsa strips are the top edges. Apply super glue gel and attach the motor box top, making sure that its edges overlap the box evenly. When set, you can putty it or not. We did not.

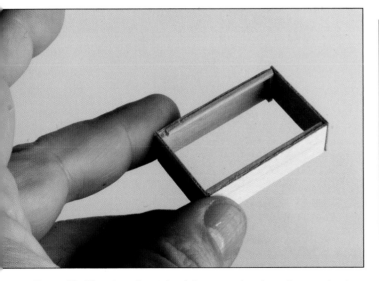

Figure 91. Glue the other side of the motor box into place so that its balsa pieces face into the motor box. Check to see that it is square and that its open edges are flush with each other.

Figure 93. Our model after its first coat of water based latex paint.

Figure 94. Our model after its third coat of paint with windows applied. These windows are the ones that were printed for the paper model. We printed them on photographic paper and then covered them with packaging tape to give them a gloss. We also backed them with double-sided carpet tape before we cut them out to make them self-adhesive. Putting windows on a boat is akin to putting eyes into the drawing of a face.

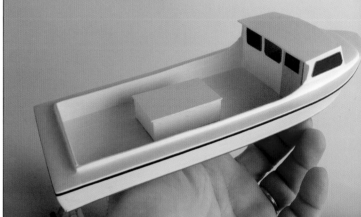

Figure 96. It is a model now.

Figure 95. Striping tape being applied to create the rub rail, so prominent in the ANNIE BUCK's appearance. The same tape will be used to mask the bottom of the hull so that green paint can be applied.

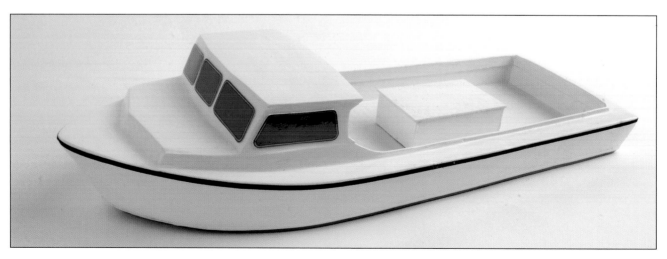

Figure 97. Another shot from the Port Bow

Chapter 16
Understanding Lines Drawings

Or, It's All in How You Slice It...

Whenever you have a shape that lacks sharp points to measure from, is rounded instead of flat, and with curvature changes throughout its body, you have something that requires additional descriptive techniques above and beyond those of the typical 3-view drawing. Such an object could be the fuselage of an airplane, the body of an aerodynamically designed car, or even the body of a person. Boat hulls are perhaps the oldest of human inventions that fit this category. This is where we will see that, while a 3-view drawing provides you with a lot of information, in its standard form it doesn't cover the kind of information needed to make a compound curved hull. Those types of drawings we cover here are based upon the same principles and really are just an expansion of the information that we have already developed.

The sheerline, chines, and keel play a large part in defining the shape of a hull. Using these components, a nice looking drawing can be made using the 3-view method.

Something is lacking, though. The issue regards what occurs between those lines, such things as flare, tumblehome, and the crowning of decks. To understand the solutions, it helps to clearly understand the dilemma. That problem is: when you have an object with such dynamic curvature as a boat, how do you measure it? The measurements of a hull are different from inch to inch to inch, depending upon where you look. Trying to really understand the shape of the boat's hull from this drawing, the way it is, is almost like trying to imagine infinity. Any measurements taken from any different points will yield very different results. The solution to this problem lies in determining where we have straight lines and using them to define reliable measuring points to build a system that makes all of the information

in between manageable. This results in what are known as **lines drawings**. Lines drawings are mechanical drawings of the lines and contours of a boat's hull.

Figure 1. The "Annie Buck" has a beautifully contoured hull for the purposes of this discussion. *Courtesy of David and Ann Phillips.*

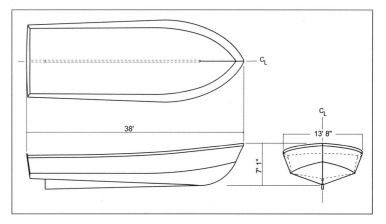

Figure 2. If we use the standard 3-view drawing technique, we end up with a very nice drawing.

This is where any reliable straight lines become important to us. There are two that are present for all boats, whether or not they are visible. One is the waterline, shown as W sub L. The other is the centerline which is shown as C sub L. Both of these lines also represent planes, which can be thought of as slicing through the body of the hull at their respective positions.

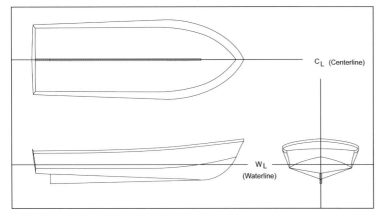

Figure 3. The waterline and centerline are straight lines. In the top view, points on the boat can be measured outwards from the centerline. In the front view, points on the boat can be measured above or below, relative to the waterline. In the end view, both kinds of measurement can be made.

The foundation that makes measurement of hulls with compound curves possible is an understanding that these two lines/planes provide the basis from which all other measuring points are derived. Once they are established, the rest of the system of measurements is built upon them. These lines have been marked on your paper model: the waterline is marked by a green line and the centerline is marked by a red line.

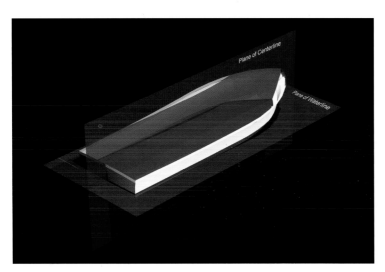

Figure 4. The waterline and centerline are not just lines, but also represent planes that split the hull. The plane of the waterline divides everything that is above or below water. The centerline plane divides the port from the starboard side.

Beneath the hull of the boat, we draw a line the length of the hull that is parallel to the waterline. This is called the **baseline**. This line is graduated in the same way as a ruler, at regularly spaced intervals, the distances being determined as required for the particular boat. The measurement ticks on the baseline are called station points. They are commonly spaced at 4- or 5-foot intervals for boats in the 30 to 50 foot range. The distances between stations may or may not be equal, but if not, they are otherwise marked. Each station mark is numbered from station zero to the highest needed. **Station points** mark the positions directly below station lines.

Note that station 0 is set at the point where the waterline meets the keel at the bow. Numbering runs toward the stern. Since we are viewing the boat from the starboard side, this means that station numbers increase going from right to left. Station points moving towards the bow are given negative numbers. This is a convention used by Naval Architects and we will use it to familiarize you with the classical method. If you are making drawings for your own use, station point zero can be placed at either end of the hull, depending upon your preferences.

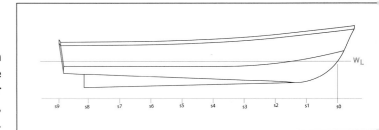

Figure 5. Using a front view, the baseline is drawn beneath the hull, so that it is parallel to the waterline. Station points are marked at intervals along the baseline. Note that in this drawing Station point zero is placed exactly below the point where the keel and waterline meet. Station numbers run towards the stern of the boat. This is standard naval architectural protocol.

A **station line** is the result of a plane that cuts across the boat, like a knife cutting a loaf of bread. If you could slice a boat, as you would a loaf of bread, then put ink on the edge of your slice and press it onto a large piece of paper, the result would be an outline of the shape of the boat at that station point. The contours of a station line are only visible in an end view. In other views it appears as a straight line. Each station line is numbered according to the number of the station point below it.

Note that when we look at an angled perspective view of the hull, there is no actual measurable information, but we can certainly get a more complete sense of the shape of it when we can see the lines of the stations compared to the 3-view drawing above.

In front or top views, stations appear only as straight lines. Even so, they are important because the points where they intersect sheerlines, chines, keel, etc. can be measured exactly relative to the points where they intersect either the waterline or the centerline. For an example, say that you want to know what the freeboard (height of the deck over the waterline) is at station 5. You can simply measure along the number 5 station line from the waterline up to the sheerline to get your answer. You can do the same with the keel and chines. If you want to know the width of the boat at the same station, go to the top view and measure from the centerline out to the sheerline and multiply your result by 2.

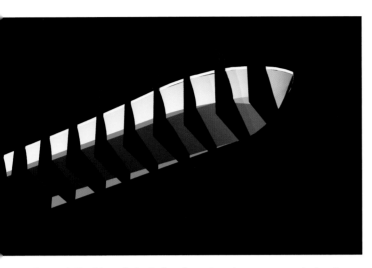

Figure 6. By "slicing" the hull with station planes, we can derive the exact contours of the hull at locations determined by station points. The resulting lines are station lines, which are most evident in an end view of the boat.

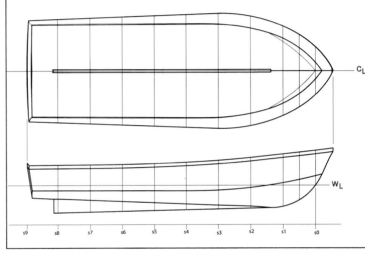

Figure 8. Station lines applied to the front and top views of a hull provide measuring points every time they intersect another line. This means that we can now measure distances between established points. For example, if we want to know how far it is from the sheer line to the chine at station 2, we can now do so.

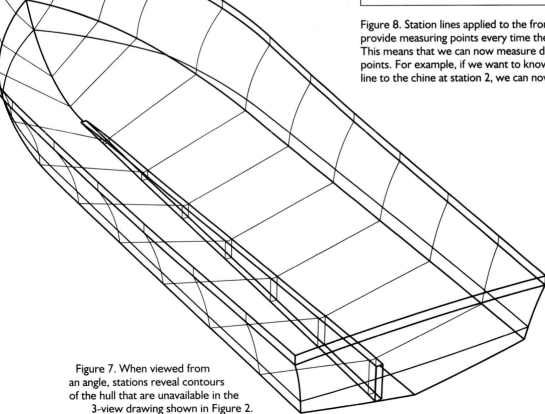

Figure 7. When viewed from an angle, stations reveal contours of the hull that are unavailable in the 3-view drawing shown in Figure 2.

Stations are most useful in the end view where they are seen as a set of curves that nest into one another. Here the curves between the sheer, the chines and the keel are made visible and become measurable. Because station lines can run close together and because each side of the hull usually mirrors the other, stations from the bow back to the widest station are shown on one side of the centerline and stations from the transom forward to that station are shown on the other. This is another method of clarifying a drawing without losing information.

Stations are set at intervals that best represent the information necessary to understand the shape of the boat. Fewer stations with larger distances between them may reduce the accuracy of information. Too many stations may provide more information than necessary and can result in drawings that are difficult to read. In certain parts of a hull that have greater shape change, such as increased compound curvature in a bow area, extra stations may be drawn to provide additional information, as in the half stations S-0.5 and S 0.5, shown in Figure 9.

In the same manner that we slice vertically with station planes that are perpendicular to the centerline, we can slice vertically and parallel to the centerline and we can slice horizontally with secondary waterlines. Each slicing method shows lines that are dramatic in one particular view, and as straight lines in the other two. In this case, it is the top view, where waterlines have their most dramatic view.

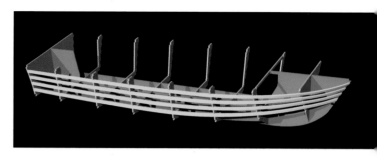

Figure 10, Looking at the structural elements of this plank on bulk-head frame, you can see how station line information is important to its design.

Secondary waterlines are planes that are parallel to the waterline and are evenly spaced above and below it. In the same way that station lines are formed by the intersections of station planes and the hull body, waterlines are formed by the intersections of secondary waterline planes and the hull body. Waterlines appear as straight lines in front and end views, but reveal the hull's shape in a top view. Again, when seen from a perspective view, waterlines reveal a lot about a hull's shape compared to the same view without. Waterlines are the basis for horizontal lift-built model construction.

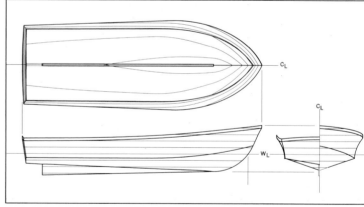

Figure 11. Secondary waterlines slice the hull horizontally. This method of "slicing" is historically important in the design of ships. In model making, it is the basis for lift-built model construction.

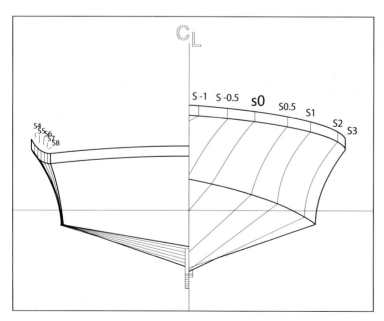

Figure 9. In the end view, station lines reveal the considerable amount of curvature of this hull. Theoretically, if we know the distances between each station curve, we have all of the information necessary to recreate the shape of the hull. Station contours form the basis for designing the structures of plank on bulkhead models. You could use the lines in this image to design bulkheads.

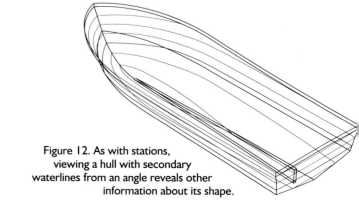

Figure 12. As with stations, viewing a hull with secondary waterlines from an angle reveals other information about its shape.

Buttock planes are planes that are parallel to the centerline and repeated at regular intervals from the centerline outwards. The buttock lines that are created at the intersection of the buttock planes and the hull body form lines that can, very dramatically, show contours of the hull when seen from the front view. Again, when seen from a perspective view, our ability to envision the shape of the hull is enhanced over the 3-view image.

Figure 13. This type of lift-built model, which is mirrored by a similar structure, was designed using secondary waterlines. Each layer of wood is referred to as a lift. In this model the lowest group of lifts are half the thickness of the upper ones. This allows for greater precision, but requires more elaborate design and cutting work. Parts of the sides were only .03125" thick when the carving of it was finished, which is unusual for this type of model.

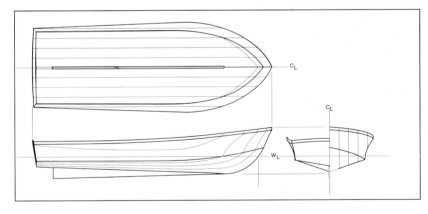

Figure 14. Buttock lines slice the hull parallel to the plane of the centerline. Buttock line contours are revealed in the front view. Note the sharp kinks where they meet the chines on this hull.

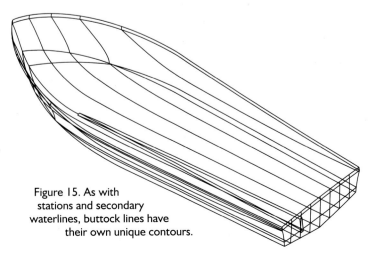

Figure 15. As with stations and secondary waterlines, buttock lines have their own unique contours.

When we combine stations, waterlines, and buttocks to a drawing that includes the sheerline, chines, and keel, we have a very descriptive image. Every point at which any two or more of these lines intersect is a usable measuring point. No longer are we concerned with an infinite number of possible measuring points. We have a finite and practical network of points to work from.

Fairing is a technique that allows us to use line drawings more effectively. If we do not have the actual sheerline, but do know where the top ends of the stations are, we can determine its placement by fairing. Fairing can be done using a flexible stick or French Curves. See more about Fairing in Chapter 10.

Obtaining data to make your own line drawings is done by measuring a boat, which is discussed in Chapter 17.

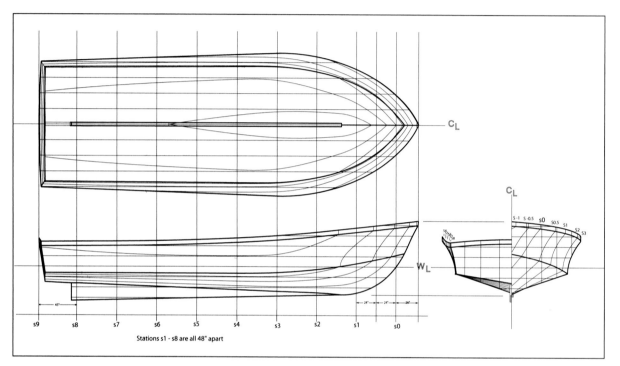

Figure 16. A tremendous amount of information is provided in this lines drawing. Any point where lines intersect can be used for measurement purposes.

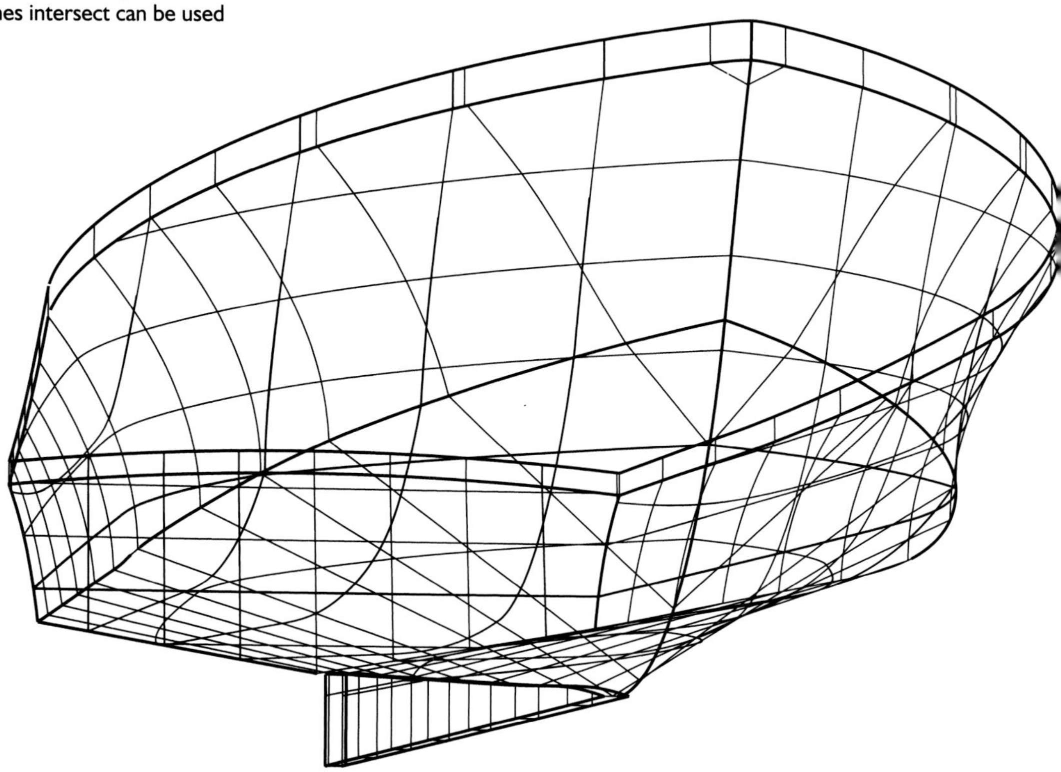

Figure 17. With experience, you will find an image like this one that shows the lines from all three "slicers" gives you a huge amount of information about the shape of the object that you are looking at.

Chapter 17

How to Measure a Boat

At this point, I would love to say "close your eyes and imagine in your mind..."

There are only a few problems, not the least of which is that you can't read with your eyes closed, so I will have to have you imagine things with your eyes open, which will be just fine. If you have a good understanding of Chapter 16, which was about lines drawings, I believe that you already know how to measure a boat, but you may not realize it yet.

I like to use graphics, photos, and illustrations as teaching tools, as you can probably tell, having read this far. For this subject, I would like to use very few, perhaps none, and have you imagine the concepts in your mind to the extent that you can. Measuring a boat is something that may take different tools and methods that work for the environment that the boat is in at a given time. Rather than tell you specifically what tools to use, since they might, or might not, be the right ones for your situation, I think that it is more important that you know what outcome needs to occur.

We will begin by discussing the hull and we can start immediately with the concept that you need to establish points on the boat that you can measure from. These points must correspond to the meeting points of stations and secondary waterlines. I generally don't use buttock lines during the measurement of boats.

As with lines drawings, the waterline and centerline are of critical importance. All secondary waterlines must be parallel to the waterline.

When we try to measure from a point on the hull of the boat to its centerline, in what seems like the obvious way, there is a serious impediment. It's the hull, itself. You cannot pass your tape measure through the side of the boat to get to it.

This is where I would have told you to close your eyes, if I could. Keep them open. Imagine the boat in your living room. I know, mine isn't that big either. The room is rectangular. You have thrown out all of the furniture; you have gotten rid of any art on the walls; and, in fact,

you have sealed up all of the windows. There isn't even any carpet on the floor; somehow it turned into perfectly smooth concrete. All of the walls and floor are flat. You can decorate the ceiling, if you want.

The boat is now sitting in your living room, perfectly in the center and with the waterline perfectly level, with the walls all exactly the same distance from it. It's a good-sized living room, to be sure.

Now you approach the problem of how to measure the boat. Remember back to the baseline with its station marks. This is a line that runs on the ground under the boat's centerline. You can easily establish this line on your new floor.

A plumb bob is a weight that hangs at the bottom of a string. It is used to cause the string to hang in a straight line, so that whatever spot on the boat that you hold your string to, the weight will be over that spot on the ground. You can use a string with washers tied at the end to do the same thing.

What the heck, your living room's ruined anyway. Go ahead and make marks on the floor. Using your plumb bob, make a mark on the floor directly below the bow and below the middle of the rear of the transom. Make a straight line between those points. This straight line is your baseline. While you're at it, make a mark on your baseline directly below where the waterline meets the keel at the front of the boat. This is your station zero point.

So, now you have a wrecked living room with a boat in it and a baseline under it. It's your turn to choose what to do... How many stations do you want to have? Personally, I would usually have between a half dozen and a dozen. Whatever you decide guides the rest of the process.

Measure the distance from your station zero point to the stern and divide it by the number of stations that you've decided on. Make marks on your baseline at those distances. Each one is now a station point and you need to number them. If you need to, refer to Chapter 16, Figure 5.

From your baseline, make perpendicular lines outward at each of the station points. You only have to do it for one side of the boat, unless the other side is different.

The nice thing about a plumb bob is that you don't only have to use it to transfer points down; you can also transfer marks from the ground up to the boat by hanging it over the mark you want to transfer. For instance: station lines.

It wouldn't be right to mess up the boat, the way that you did with your living room, so I recommend using colored masking tape to make marks on the boat. Test it somewhere inconspicuous to be safe, but it is usually harmless to most surfaces.

Using your plumb bob, make a mark on the keel of the boat at each station line. Using the same method, make marks on the chines and then the sheerline at each station. At each station, run a piece of tape from the keel up to the chine and from the chine to the sheerline.

You have now created stations on the boat. Refer to Chapter 16, Figure 7.

Now, you will have to figure out where the secondary waterlines are. This is easy, because in this case, the waterline is level with the floor. This means that the secondary waterlines will also be level with the floor. The next thing to do then is to determine the height intervals between our waterlines.

We will arbitrarily decide on 12" as the distance. We need to measure the height from the waterline to the floor. Then we need to measure that distance plus 12" up from the floor, to mark the height of our first secondary waterline on each station line. It's important that our measuring tool is plumb and not angled along the side of the hull, or our measurements will be skewed.

This must be repeated at each station and for each level of waterline. We can then tape our waterlines onto the boat, as we did with our station lines. Refer to Chapter 16, Figure 12.

It's not a bad idea to place a vertical tape through the centerline of the transom, which can be done by dividing its width in half at the top and running the tape from that point to the point where the keel meets the transom.

You should now have a boat sitting in your living room with a strange matrix of lines on it.

That matrix of lines should resemble some of the images in Chapter 16, with the addition of a boat.

Every point where your tape lines come together with other tape lines is a measuring point. Every point where a line comes together with a feature, such as the chines, the keel or the sheerline, is also a measuring point.

Each of these measuring points is a certain distance to the front or rear of the boat based upon which station it falls on. The location of each station is its distance from station zero.

Each of these measuring points is a certain distance at, above or below the main waterline, based upon the waterline it falls on. The main waterline can be thought of as waterline zero.

In fact, the point at which station zero, waterline zero, and the keel come together is really the zero point of the boat, similar to the zero point in Cartesian space.

Once this is clear, we can do the rest of the measuring job, which is to take the measurements of the relationship of each measuring point from Zero.

Every measuring point is a certain distance above or below, a certain distance ahead or behind and a certain distance outward from Zero.

All measuring points that fall on waterline 1 are 12" above Zero. If our stations are 48" apart, all measuring points on station 1 are 48" to the rear of Zero and all measuring points on station 2 are 96" to the rear of zero.

We need to record the location of each measuring point. Since we know the distances of the stations and the waterlines from Zero, any intersection of those lines has two known dimensions. However, we need three dimensions to locate any point.

From this, the use of offset tables, in boat building, came about.

Figure 1 shows an offsets table. It is not traditional in its layout, but it works. If you know the height and distance forward or rearward of Zero, which is provided by the numbers corresponding to waterlines and stations, respectively, you only need the dimension outward from the centerline in the box. This particular set of offsets also has chine and sheerline information.

You may need to spend some time thinking about how this works. I know I did when I first learned how to do it, but is a good way to write down a lot of data in a small place.

Before leaving offsets tables, I want to point out that if you want to work from traditional ones, the numbers in each box will usually appear in a format something like this: 1-3-7. The way to read these numbers is that the first digit represents feet, the second inches and the third, eighths (sometimes sixteenths) of an inch. So the way to read the number would be 1' 3 7/8". I prefer to use decimal numbers myself. They fit better into the style I use for design work.

Back to the mess we made of your living room. The point is to find the locations of each of these measuring points, so that we can later make line drawings of a boat of choice. We need to determine where in space these points are relative to Zero, or a representative of Zero, such as the main waterline, station zero or the boat's centerline.

There are occasions when things aren't perfect. We can't get to the centerline, due to an obstruction, such as a trailer (or the boat is in the water), or some other impediment exists. If we can't get to the centerline, we need an outside measuring line that is parallel to the centerline. The walls of your living room are good. If we can find the distance between the wall and any point on the centerline, we can measure to measuring points on the hull from the wall and subtract that distance from the distance from the wall to the centerline.

Of course, it doesn't have to be a wall. It can be a post that is plumb moved from station to station, or other device, but I hope you understand how we can get past certain impediments.

Since I know you didn't really destroy your living room, you might want to place your paper, or wood, model into a shoe box and compare this arrangement to the ideas we have discussed.

If you are around boats a lot, you will know that the living room situation would be an "ideal" case. The problem is that boats are on trailers, they are on hills, they are in the water, etc., etc. It is more important that you understand what you need to get from the boat than that you learn a single way of doing it.

Before we leave the subject, measuring the superstructure of most boats is far more straightforward. You can measure in from the sheerline and you can get to the centerline, although you must determine where it is and clearly mark it. Interior parts of hulls are just as important as any others and you will need to measure those features as well. Stations used for designing models will need to reflect these interior areas. Station tape can be extended onto decks, into cockpits, and up the sides of superstructure houses, if necessary.

I will repeat what I said early in the book, you might end up with more information than you need about a boat. This is never a problem. You could also not collect enough; so always err on the side of caution.

When you take measurements, take copious notes. Take lots of photographs. As we saw in Chapter 12, good broadside shots can be very beneficial. The objective of such shots is to minimize distortion. When you look through your camera you should have this in mind. Shots of the stern taken from straight back are good for the same reason. I recommend that anything that will be in your model should have photographs for reference. Don't forget the tops of cabins or other high areas. What you don't see of the real boat might be something quite obvious when you reduce it to model size.

Thus, you should have photos that are specifically of the boat as a whole, reflecting the larger areas: the hull, the superstructure, the cockpit, etc. You should also have photos that are dedicated to the smaller items, such as hardware and their locations relative to other things in the boat.

We practice "photogrammetry," which is a very sophisticated group of methods based upon art perspective theory and various types of mathematics, in order to develop dimensions from photos. It has taken many years to learn and develop many of our own methods and we plan to write a book dedicated to the subject.

Measuring, as you can see, does takes some work and good organization, but there is no reason that you cannot do it, if you can understand the concepts in Chapter 16. It gives you the freedom to choose your own subject boat and to really build from scratch.

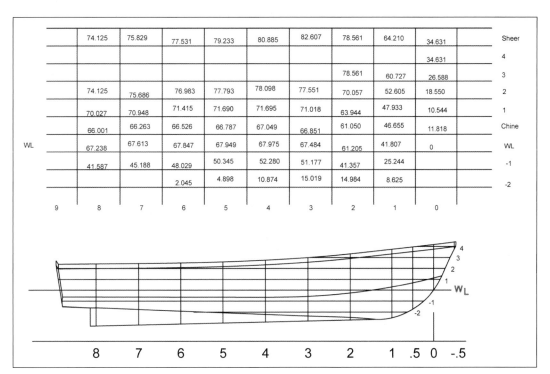

	9	8	7	6	5	4	3	2	1	0	
		74.125	75.829	77.531	79.233	80.885	82.607	78.561	64.210	34.631	Sheer
										34.631	4
								78.561	60.727	26.588	3
		74.125	75.686	76.983	77.793	78.098	77.551	70.057	52.605	18.550	2
		70.027	70.948	71.415	71.690	71.695	71.018	63.944	47.933	10.544	1
		66.001	66.263	66.526	66.787	67.049	66.851	61.050	46.655	11.818	Chine
WL		67.238	67.613	67.847	67.949	67.975	67.484	61.205	41.807	0	WL
		41.587	45.188	48.029	50.345	52.280	51.177	41.357	25.244		-1
			2.045	4.898	10.874	15.019	14.984	8.625			-2

Figure 1. I really couldn't conjure something like this in your mind without a picture. This is a type of "offsets table" and hull drawing. Note that the columns are over station lines and that there are numbers to the right of the graph denoting secondary waterlines. Based upon the notion that we know, the distance of each of the stations from zero and each of the waterlines from zero, we only need one other dimension, which is the one in the box, to know exactly where the point in question lies.

Chapter 18
Lift Building Theory

Like so many other things about boat hulls, lift building is based upon fairing. In the case of lift building, however, we are fairing as we carve. We cannot get to our measuring points until we reach down into them. Lift building is familiar to many of us, because of the odd stair step characteristics it has. How we determine where those stair steps fall and how they work may not be so familiar.

In Figure 1 we have four views of the same station of an inverted half hull. It has already been laminated and is ready for carving as is shown in Figure 1a (same image). In Figure 1b, we have added arrows to indicate our measuring points, which are the inside corners of each stair. The dotted line in Figure 4b shows how the intended hull contour runs through these points. In Figure 1c, the arrow indicates

the direction of downhill cutting relative to the wood of the lifts, as we discussed in carving theory. The cuts in Figure 1c are rough cuts that bring us close to, but not all of the way into, our measuring points. In Figure 4d, we make our finer cuts, fairing the contours as we proceed. If we cut all of the way to the measuring points in 4c we would risk taking off material at points where the hull is convex. If you wish you can check the fair of your carving by using a thin strip of wood as you would in other circumstances.

How do we arrive at our lines for lift building?

We start by working backwards. We need to know what the finished project looks like first and then determine what needs to be done to achieve it.

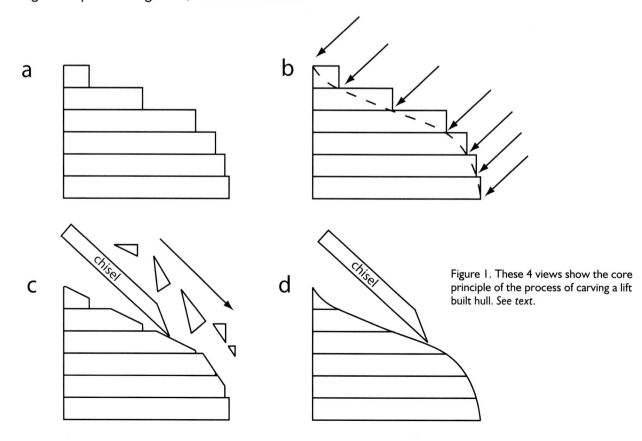

Figure 1. These 4 views show the core principle of the process of carving a lift built hull. *See text.*

This is akin to what historically would have been working forward. When boats were designed by using lift built models, the first step was to carve a block made from lifts that were pinned together, but not glued. The shape of the carved model would be the boat's shape. In order to determine what the dimensions for the boat would be, the lifts were separated and the outlines of them would provide secondary waterlines. These dimensions would then be scaled up in a complex process known as "lofting."

Whatever type of model you want to make, the principles for building a half hull or any other lift built model are the same. If you are not building interior features, do not design them into your model. If you are planning to build a half hull, simply make one side of the hull and attach to a suitable backing board.

The example in Figure 2 is a plank on lift-built model. This means that the final carving is meant to be covered with planks.

This model has three cockpits and an engine compartment, thus its interior features would be considered pretty detailed for a lift built model. Since we are only discussing construction of the hull, we are only concerned with structure that is below the sheerline. Because planks are applied to the exterior, as in plank on bulkhead construction, we would reduce all exterior dimensions inward by the thickness of the planks, just as we would with any structural form that is covered with outer planks.

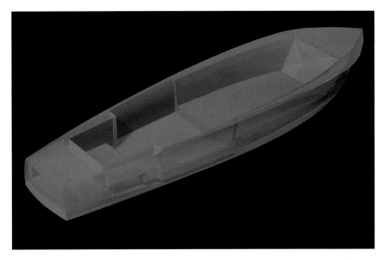

Figure 3. A transparent block with the shape of the structure we need to build.

If we add a few of the parts planned for the model, you can begin to see how things will shape up.

This is an instance where thinking additively works well. When we work additively, we are making assemblies from smaller parts. Carving, milling or any other technique that removes material from a larger single piece is a subtractive technique.

Bear in mind that we are laminating pieces that will result in a solid structure for the basis of the hull, but the thin bulkheads, upholstery and bits of trim cannot be carved from this same piece, even by the best of carvers. This means our job is to create the right type of space for the things that we will be adding into it. How do we best plan for interior space? Let's return our block to its more realistic wood composition.

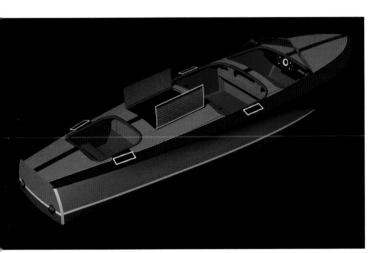

Figure 2. This picture shows what kind of boat the lifts we are discussing are designed for.

The first question is, what is the basic structure that we need? Through the magic of computers, we have a transparent image of the shape of the hull structure that fits our needs. Actually, this rendering is the result of several months of work and did not occur magically.

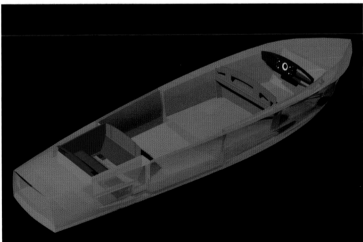

Figure 3b. Separation of compartments and other internal features do not have to be part of the lift building process. In this case, bulkheads, wall liners, and flooring material are added to the hull later.

Be sure to factor in your experience and carving abilities when deciding what features to include in the lifts and which features to construct separately.

This model will have three cockpits. What are the structural features of those cockpits? We are not concerned with the smaller hardware in this question. We need to know what will come into contact with our block and what will be installed into our block. In the first cockpit we have sidewalls, flooring, both flat and angled, a dashboard, and a seat. The dashboard will be mounted to the deck, so we don't need to worry about it. The second cockpit is separated by a thin bulkhead with glove box cabinetry. It also has sidewalls, flat flooring, a seat, and another thin bulkhead that separates it from the motor box. The engine compartment will house the engine and its various accessories. The third cockpit is separated from it by another thin bulkhead with sloped flooring at the bottom and some other trim features. It also has sidewalls and another seat.

These are all of the interior features that we must make accommodations for. In the same way that we must modify our dimensions to account for the thickness of exterior planking, we need to do the same to accommodate for thicknesses of any sidewalls and/or any added flooring.

Inside the motor compartment, where the appearance will be that of painted wood, we are not adding walls and so we don't have to make any changes from our original dimensions. This is important because our lifts in that area will be very thin already. Making them thinner only makes things more fragile and difficult during carving.

Although this discussion is not about deck building, we should explain that the shape of the top of our block will provide an excellent base for virtually any type of deck structure that might be used, because there is a very large amount of sturdy surface area to mount parts to.

This type of construction does require quite a large amount of wood, relative to plank on frame or plank on bulkhead construction, and results in a significantly heavier model. It is not a great method for R/C construction, although it's is not unheard of. Because of the increased weight and the distribution of it, balance could be a potential problem. For those wishing to make R/C boats from fiberglass, however, it is an excellent method for constructing a plug for casting, in which case there is no need to worry about the interior at all. In fiberglass construction, the hull is hollow and any interior parts are added in.

The outlines of the lifts are determined by using the waterlines from a lines drawing. Figure 5 shows what happens when we add "slicers," the planes that separate the hull at each secondary waterline.

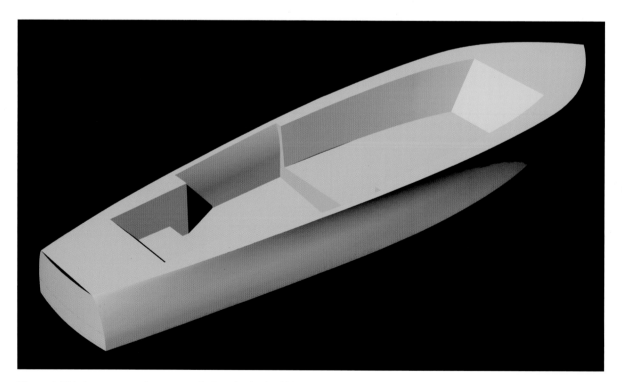

Figure 4. This is a more realistic view of what the finished block should look like.

When we remove the slicers and separate the lifts, we see a collection of somewhat odd shapes:

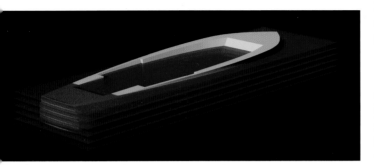

Figure 5. Slicers show where we split the hull when we determine secondary waterlines.

Looking at them from the bottom, does not make them any less odd.

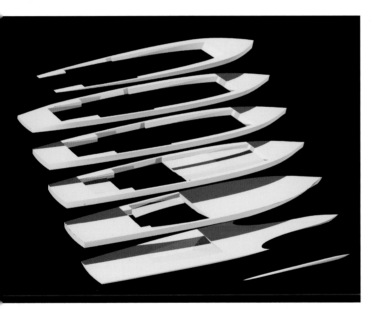

Figure 6. The lifts that remain when the slicers are removed have an odd appearance.

Don't let these shapes intimidate you. Making them, while not exactly simple, is not nearly as bad as it looks. Remember, these are separations of a single unit that was laminated and was already carved, not separately made pieces. You will never see these pieces in this way unless you only pin your laminations together and don't glue them. Remember that we are looking at the process in reverse.

Except for the top and bottom lifts, every one is touched by two slicers. This is very important to bear in mind. This means that each lift's outlines are determined by the waterline above it and the waterline below it. To demonstrate what this means we will isolate one of the lifts for analysis.

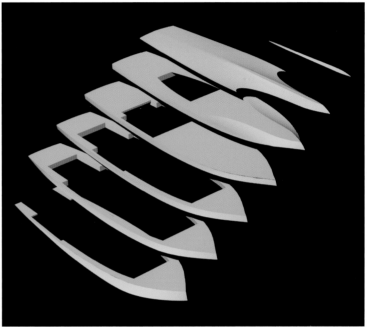

Figure 7. Their shapes are also odd looking and really quite complex when seen from the bottom as well.

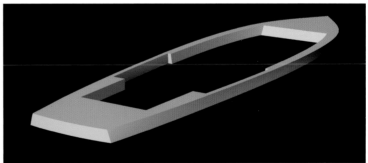

Figure 8. This is the third lift down from the top.

Reducing the lift in Figure 8 to its lines, we see the following angles and shapes that must be carved.

Looking at Figure 9, note that in the stern this boat has tumblehome, which you will remember is when the sides of the boat get narrower as you go upward from chines to the sheerline. This boat also has flare in the bow, which is the opposite; the boat widens as you move up from the chines to the sheerline.

I was once told by a well respected boat builder that any boat that has flare in the bow and tumblehome in the stern also has a "crossover" point. This is a point where tumblehome must reverse angle to become flare and it is essentially a vertical straight line. I don't know the necessary science to say whether or not this is always so, but so far it has worked for us and you are about to see its significance.

Interplay between upper and lower waterlines in the shape of a lift:

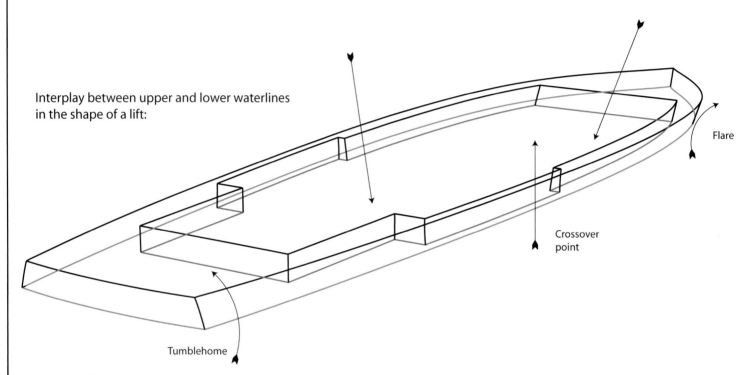

Flare

Crossover point

Tumblehome

Figure 9. This image contains information that illustrates the importance of using both the top and bottom waterlines when determining the outlines of lifts.

In Figure 10, we have the same lift from as viewed from above. It illustrates the point that I am making here about paying attention to both waterlines. If you try to use a single waterline as your pattern you will not have the wood necessary to make the whole part. If you use the red, or lower, waterline in this image, you will not have the wood necessary to make the flare of the bow, which falls outside its boundaries. Conversely, if you use the upper waterline, shown in black, you will have omitted material needed for not only the tumblehome, but the forward interior slopes, as well. The value of the crossover point is that it marks the point on the exterior lines where the outline you use changes from bottom to top. Give this information a moment to sink in. It's very important.

The following rule will always get you by:

Always use whichever is the outermost line of the two waterlines for the exterior of the lift outline and always use whichever is the innermost line of the two waterlines for the interior of the lift's outline.

This is true for all lifts.

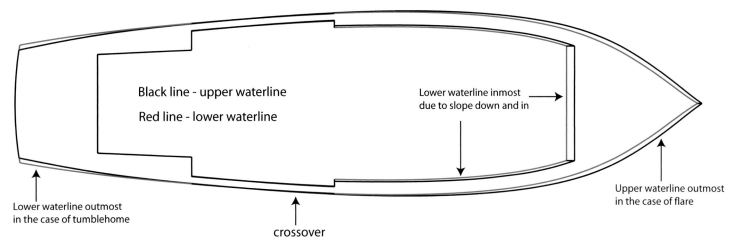

Black line - upper waterline

Red line - lower waterline

Lower waterline inmost
due to slope down and in

Upper waterline outmost
in the case of flare

Lower waterline outmost
in the case of tumblehome

crossover

Figure 10. Each waterline misses areas that belong to the other. If, for example, the lower waterline was used alone for marking the outline of the lift, there would not be enough wood to cut the bow from.

In the case of those lifts that incorporate the sheerline, it needs to be understood that there is no longer an upper waterline to serve as the top boundary. It is replaced by the sheerline, which will usually be at an angle relative to the plane of the waterlines. By marking the sheerline well on those pieces, one can avoid accidentally removing too much wood. Note that when there is tumblehome, lines need to be added on top of the deck to mark the sheerline to the rear of the crossover point; the sheerline will be inside the boundaries of the lift.

From the side, mark the lines of the chines. You can determine the measurements from the front view of the line drawing you use. To obtain a smooth line fair your measuring points with a thin strip of wood. It may help to enlist an extra pair of hands to do this.

This is what the total sum of the block of lifts should look like before carving:

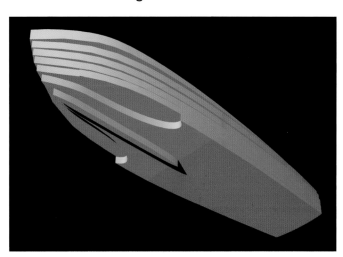

Figure 12. All lifts assembled prior to any carving as seen from the bottom.

Figure 11. Lifts that incorporate the sheer line don't have a top waterline. The sheer line replaces the top waterline in that function. The width shown for the top outline occurs at the height of the sheer line.

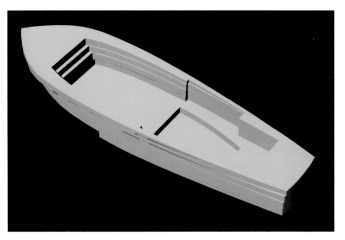

Figure 13. All lifts assembled prior to any carving as seen from the top.

Although it is a somewhat awesome sight to see all of the lifts together this way I am going to make some strong recommendations. Learned the hard way over a long period of time, here they are:

• Cut each lift as two pieces. One reason that you would find out soon enough is that it is problematic to maneuver such pieces in any saw, not to mention that you would have to cut through the side of your piece to get into the middle.

• Design each lift pair as two lengthwise halves. The primary reason for this is that it is almost impossible to make two cuts of this type that are exactly matched. Take two planks that are the proper thickness for your lift and secure them in alignment with double sided tape. Then cut them together. After you make your cut, you can then separate them in butterfly fashion and assign one to the port side of the boat and the other to the starboard.

• Another reason to use halves is that it is very difficult to clamp the whole hull down for carving. It is not nearly as difficult to do with one side at a time. Working each side separately lets you compare your carving results in ways that you cannot do when it is in one piece.

• I also recommend that you include alignment pin holes in your patterns and drill them before you cut your wood. Pinning assures that your lifts are aligned properly before carving.

• We use pins made of 1/16" piano wire. Make them longer than the total thickness of your planks, because they must be removed before any carving takes place. Piano wire will destroy the edge of any type of cutting tool that hits it.

• We recommend using polyurethane glue, which foams and fills any irregularities in the wood and is easy to remove when dry. Our next choice would be type II carpenter's glue, which is very strong, yet carvable.

There is a lot of information in this chapter. You may want to reread it one or more times to really digest it. Once you understand it, along with how to understand lines drawings and how carving theory works, you have the knowledge you need to make a hull of this type.

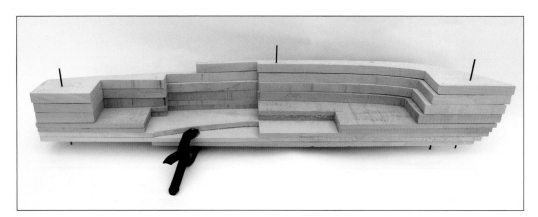

Figure 14. This is a similar set of lifts, cut in halves and pinned, but not yet glued. Note the similarities to the subject hull in this chapter. Note also, that in this case, where more detail is needed, some of the lifts are half the thickness of the others. This is similar to the concept of half stations that we discussed in Chapter 16.

Figure 15. Note the position and direction of cut, which is downhill relative to the grain of the wood. The grain of this wood, which is basswood, is pretty close to parallel with the centerline of the hull.

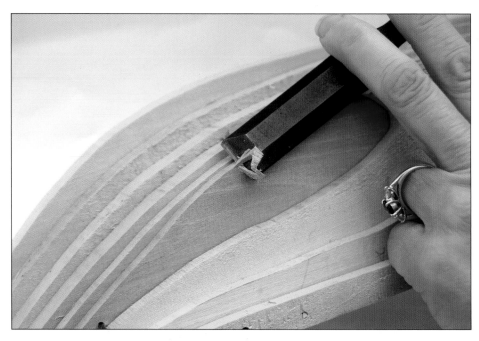

Chapter 19
Plank on Bulkhead Theory

One of the most popular and practical ways of making model boats is by using the plank on bulkhead method. This method results in a lighter model with no constraints on how interior space can be laid out. Compared with lift building, it may or may not be an easier method to convert conceptually from marine drawings to model construction, depending upon how you prefer to work. Many people are familiar with this type of construction, because the vast majority of model boat kits use some variation of it.

For R/C, plank on bulkhead is one of the best construction types there is. If that is your purpose, make sure that all of your adhesives and all of your finishes will be waterproof. You don't want to make a gorgeous model that falls apart in the water.

A good way to gain an understanding of any type of model construction is to look at the process in reverse.

The reason that we look at the construction of the boat in reverse is that we need to know what will have to be built before we build it. When we design our own models, we make an image of the boat as it will be when it is finished. This corresponds with the information provided in marine drawings available by measuring from the intersections of stations, buttocks, and waterlines, as well as their intersections with the hull's measurement features. Our objective with any type of hull construction is that it provides a sturdy body or framework to support the external surfaces of the model and provides necessary attachment points for other structures the model will have.

By examining the boat in reverse, we are looking first at the things that will require the support of the hull's structure, such as panels, planking or just a coat of paint. We are also viewing the dimensional limits of where the hull structure must be and cannot be.

At the moment, we are concentrating on the hull's design, and we need to limit our focus to its shape and those things that cause that shape to be what it is. Let's remove parts of the boat, layer by layer. The bottom level of the deck is flush with the top of the hull structure and we can remove all of it. All of the seats, the motor box, and other interior features are attached to the floor and/or side walls, which are very thin and flexible plywood with a covering material. This means they are not part of the floor and can be removed from the image, as well.

Let's also remove the port side structures, for clarity.

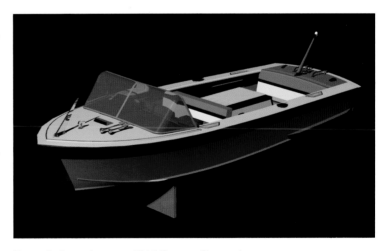

Figure 1. Our subject is a 1964 Century Coronado.

The locations of the exterior surfaces of the boat are obvious. The interior walls also mark the location of interior extents of the sides.

The bulkheads are the vertical transverse flat pieces that look like stations. In fact, they are cut to the outlines of the boat's stations in their respective positions. If you can establish the shapes of a boat's stations, you can make bulkheads. See Chapter 16. The outside edges of the bulkheads must be reduced by the thickness of the side planks.

The locations of the floor and interior walls determine the interior outlines of each bulkhead. Again, we must subtract the thickness of the walls and the thickness of the floor from that amount or we will have an error when trying to install them.

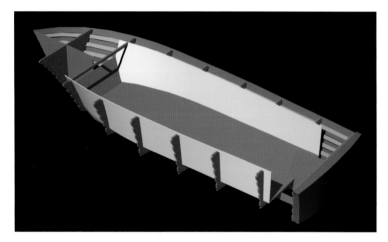

Figure 2. We have removed all interior structures, the deck, and port exterior wall for clarity.

The transom of this boat has a considerable curve to it, so we have chosen to carve the arc into a thicker piece of wood. This means that it can be removed from the hull structure during this analysis. We will also remove the interior walls.

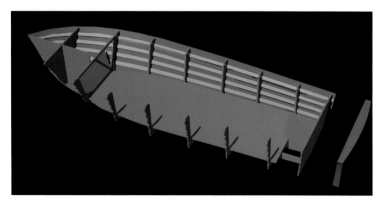

Figure 3. With the transom and interior walls removed, we can see how the flooring parts mesh with the rest of the structure more clearly. Note the stringers on the interior of the starboard side.

We can now see the inside of the exterior of the port side of the boat. Note the lighter thinner pieces of wood; they are called stringers.

We will remove the floor and turn the boat so that we are observing from the starboard side. We have also removed all but one plank. Note that the plank's edges line up with the centers of the stringers.

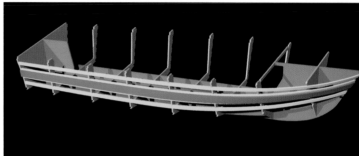

Figure 4. Looking from the starboard side. We have removed all but one plank to show that its edges line up with the centers of the stringers that back it up.

If we remove that plank we will see how the stringers line up. All of the small notches in the bulkheads that you see here, including at the corners, are meant to have some type of stringer. We like to use stringers that are wider than they are thick. The planks are glued to the stringers, usually with a super-glue gel type of cement and wider stringers provide better surface area for better adhesion. Bear in mind that the planks on a model of this type are bent significantly and may not want to adhere, because they don't like to bend.

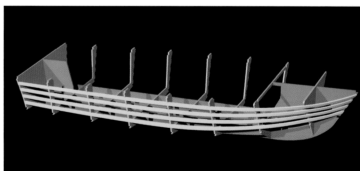

Figure 5. The remaining plank has been removed to show the even spacing of the stringers, as well as their width.

To determine the locations of stringer notches on your bulkheads, measure the length of the side of the bulkhead that you are applying the planks to. Determine the number of planks that you will be using and divide the length of that edge by the number of planks. Then use dividers or calipers to mark the mid-point of each notch. The notch should be as deep as the thickness of your stringer and the same width as your stringer.

When the stringers are removed all we have are stations and buttocks... Oops, I mean bulkheads, a keel, and secondary keels. These parts are the manifestation of stations and buttocks.

With only the bulkheads showing, it is possible to imagine the parts to come. Their spacing, if you used the original stations from your lines drawing, should be the same as on the lines drawing at the scale you are working with. This is how you know where to put them relative to your keel.

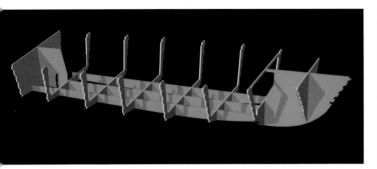

Figure 6. When all we have are bulkheads and keels, it is similar to having stations and buttocks. Compare this image to the information shown in a drawing such as Figure 16 in Chapter 16.

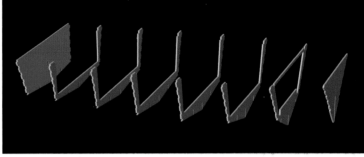

Figure 8. The spacing between the bulkheads is the same as the spacing in the line drawing they come from. Even isolated from the other parts of their boat, you can imagine the shape of it when they are properly positioned.

The keel's outside edge conforms to the keel as seen in a lines drawing, again with the exception that we must account for the thickness of exterior planking. The top and inside cuts of the keel are based upon where the floor and any other features of the type would go.

The same factors are true for the secondary keels, except that instead of being designed on the lines of the keel, they are designed along the lines of one of the buttocks. Their purpose is to stabilize and align the bulkheads that cross them. Bulkheads that are only singly attached at the keel tend to be hard to keep square to the keel, which can play havoc with all of the dimensions of the boat from that point on.

There are two principle types of joinery involved in making plank on bulkhead structures. The first is the notch joint, which we already discussed for our stringer notches. The second is the key to assembling such a model: it is the slip-joint. Where bulkheads meet keels, you will see long notches, one on the keel, the other, from the opposite direction, in the bulkhead. They should be self-explanatory, but be sure that their width is the same as that of the adjoining piece and that you make the cuts in each piece come from the opposite direction. It helps to set a rule for yourself that all cuts in the keels will be from the top and all cuts in the bulkheads will come from the bottom. When you standardize things this way, it helps to reduce problems.

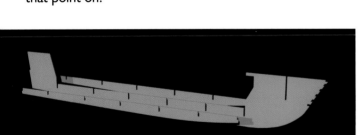

Figure 7. Keel and secondary keels isolated. Secondary keels follow the lines of buttocks. The keel is the keel.

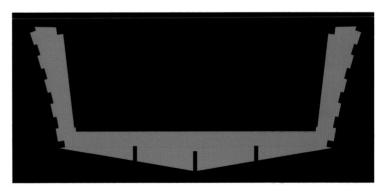

Figure 9. A single bulkhead: Here you can see the station profile on its outside edges. Other features are the various notches for stringers, an indent where the floor will sit, and the long notches for the "slip-joints;" the points where it will interface with the keel and secondary keels.

Chapter 20
Gallery

Here are some of the over 300 models that we have made over the years.

This is Tom Donley's 1958 Century Coronado *RETROSPECT*.

Figures 1 through 2. *RETROSPECT.* 1":1' scale. Length 21". Plank on lift built construction. *Courtesy of Tom Donley.*

This is a 30' pleasure trawler.

Figures 3 through 5. 30' trawler *Periwinkle*.
.5":1' scale. Length 15". Lift built hull.

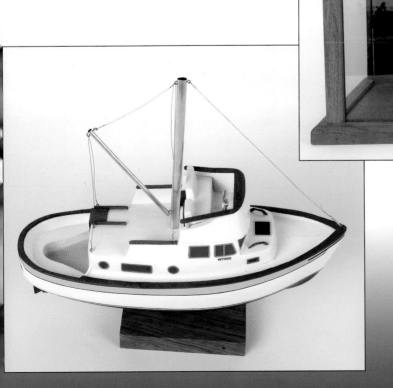

1959 Century Coronado *THE WRIGHT CHOICE.*

Figures 6 through 11. 1959 Century Coronado, *THE WRIGHT CHOICE.* 1":1' scale. Length 21". Plank on lift built construction. *Courtesy of John Wright.*

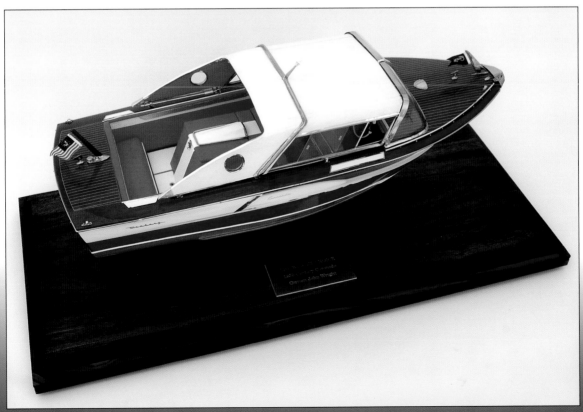

Figures 12 through 18, (pp.152-154). *Happie* is a 39' raised deck cruiser built in 1932 in Portland, Connecticut. The model is .5":1' scale. Lift built hull. *Courtesy of Dan and Kathy Wilson.*

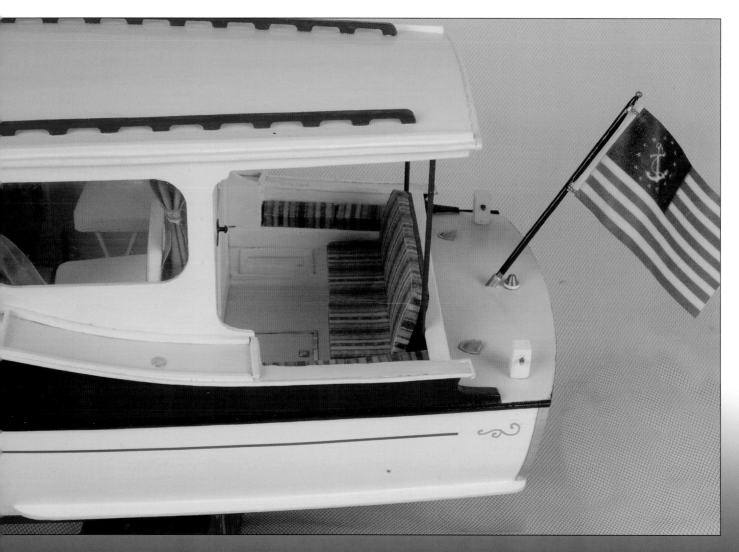

HAPPIE is a 39' raised deck cruiser.

1964 Century Coronado.

Figures 19 through 25, (pp.155-157). 1964 Century Coronado. 1.5":1' scale. Length 31.5" Plank on bulkhead construction. *Courtesy of Robert Green Jr.*

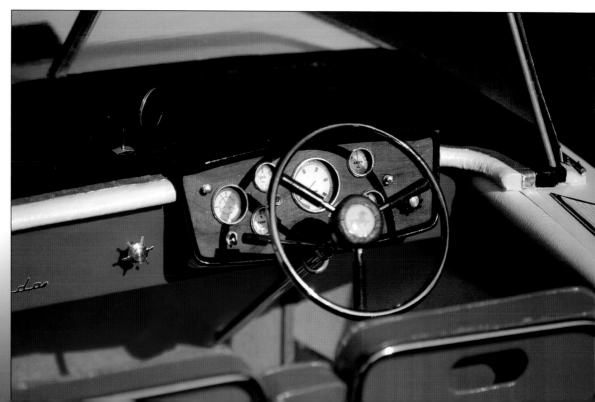

The *Marsc-Hen*, a 30' Modern cabin cruiser.

Figures 26 through 29. The *Marsc-Hen*: A modern 30' cabin cruiser. Experimental hull construction. *Courtesy of Carl Baxter.*

And finally, for this book, a few more shots of my great
uncle Grover Into's beautiful, unidentified half-hull.

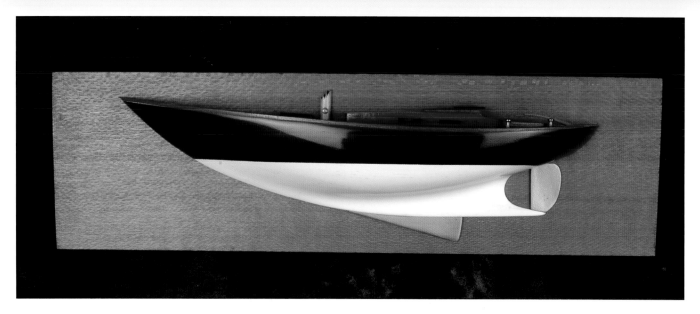

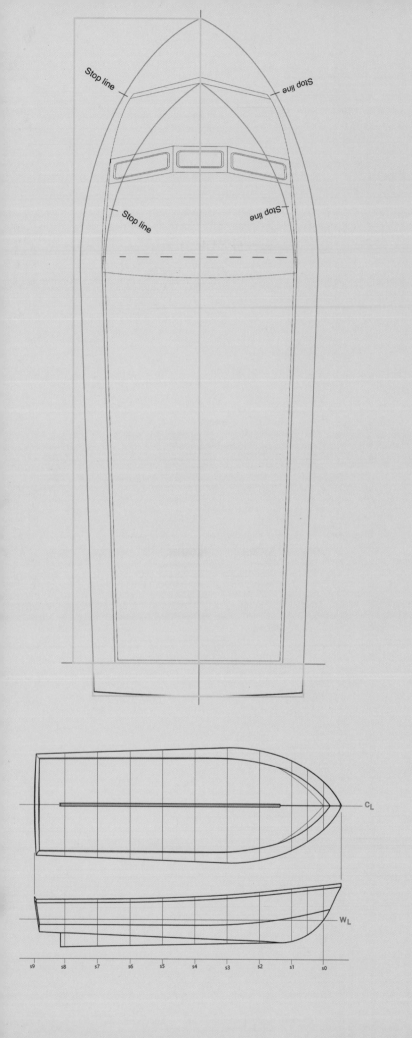

Stop line

Stop line

Stop line

Stop line

C_L

W_L

s9   s8   s7   s6   s5   s4   s3   s2   s1   s0